Ebony's Legacy: Book 1 and Book 2

Book 2: The Legacy Continues

Dawn Carr

Published by Dawn Carr, 2024.

This is a work of fiction. Similarities to real people, places, or events are entirely coincidental.

EBONY'S LEGACY: BOOK 1 AND BOOK 2

First edition. July 5, 2024.

Copyright © 2024 Dawn Carr.

ISBN: 979-8894010250

Written by Dawn Carr.

DEDICATION

To my children, Dalton, Evan, James Alton, Adelyn, and Anastasia. It took me over twenty years to finally get the courage to finish this book. I knew I needed to be an example to all of you so that you can follow your dreams. Do not live in fear. Spread your wings.

To my sweet husband, thank you for always believing in me and supporting me when I do not believe in myself. I love you. I love you with all my heart and soul.

Chapter 1
Faith

Faith Edwards was lying in the grass beside the creek. It felt damp against her skin. The grass was as green as her eyes, and the yellow wildflowers made her happy as she plucked one and placed it behind her ear. She could hear Maw Sally calling her name, but she was not ready to go home just yet. She needed some time to think about how she was going to handle the situation with her father, or Papa as she called him. Maw Sally was calling her name again. Faith knew if she did not hurry up and go back up to the house, she would get an ear full from her. Faith sat up and grunted as she put her boots on, mumbling under her breath. She could stay at her favorite spot forever.

Maw Sally was a petite, tiny, spitfire of a woman. She had dark skin, white hair that was covered with a wrap. She had been in Faith's life since before she was born. She was a nursemaid to Faith's mother, Alexandria, who died while birthing Faith. Maw Sally is the only real mother Faith has ever known. Maw Sally was on the front porch when she saw Faith walking up from the backfields. "Chile you out there daydreaming again?" Maw Sally already knew the answer to this question.

"Yes ma'am," Faith said with a smirk.

"Child, you know you must be careful doing that now. You is a grown woman and do not need to be off gallivanting by yourself. It is dangerous," Maw Sally scolded.

Faith tilted her head slightly as she was walking up the dusty wood steps, "Now, Maw Sally, you know I can take care of myself. Papa taught me himself."

Maw Sally shook her head and knew there was no use in arguing. "Well, go on upstairs, and I will draw you a bath. I have already boiled the water, and it is ready. Hurry along.

Faith bounded up the stairs into her room with the adjoining washroom that was private from the rest of the house. Her room was spacious with a canopy bed her Papa had custom-built for her. It was dark mahogany with chiffon-draped coverings. The mattress was a soft featherbed mattress. Her floors were pristine hardwood and were a lighter contrast to the bed. She walked into the adjoining room where her white claw foot tub stood in all its glory. Faith dropped off her dress and apron and climbed into the warm bath. It felt heavenly on her pale white skin. Her hair hung over the end of the tub in a cascade, not quite reaching the floor. The only thing that would make this any better was bubbles, which, of course, she forgot. Faith dreaded the dinner tonight at the house. She hated the commotion of all the guests coming in. She did not like meeting suitors. She did not need to be married off. She was fine and liked her life just the way it was. She knew that she had to talk to her father in private. Soon.

Maw Sally hurried into the bathroom at full speed, "Child, we got to get you up and running. The guests will be here before you know it!"

Faith opened her eyes and sat up in the tub, "Why do we have to be in such a hurry? Why do I have to be there, anyway? You know how I hate being around those types."

"Never mind that child. Your father wants you there," Maw Sally said as she started drying her hair. "Now get out of this tub so we can get you ready now, young lady!"

Faith stared at her reflection in the mirror as she put the final changes on her hair. Flaming red hair fell around her face in curls and her long locks were pulled back. Her eyes looked like two emeralds, which matched her dark green velvet gown. Her gown was low, and her breast showed ample cleavage but not too much. The gown was straight and reached her toes. She pinched her cheeks to give them some color and stood to get ready to go downstairs. As she reached to open the door, she thought again, I must speak to Papa.

Faith descended slowly down the stairs. She walked with deliberate slow steps, as she was not looking forward to being around these people. She dreaded having to be around her cousin, Louis. He made her skin crawl. She could never figure out why she did not feel comfortable around him, but she never had. He just seemed very odd. Faith could hear the sounds of conversations coming from the parlor. She reached the bottom of the stairs and took a right into the parlor. As she slowly entered the doorway, she could see the piano in the far corner. A woman from the bank, where her father worked, was busy playing some melody that Faith did not recognize. To the left in front of the window was her father, whispering with a few men. He saw her as she entered. "Faith, come and let me introduce you to my colleagues!"

Faith smiled politely and took her father's hand.

"Faith, this is Dexter Scott. He is a banker that I just hired at Edwards Banking."

Dexter took Faith's hand and brought it to his lips. Faith had to choke back the bile that rose in the back of her throat.

"Nice to meet you sir," Faith said through a forced smile.

Dexter let his eyes slowly slide up her arm to her breast where they lingered and then up to her eyes and said, "The pleasure is all mine, dear. All mine."

Mr. Edwards cleared his throat, as if to be uncomfortable and interrupt this exchange. "This other gentleman is a colleague of Mr. Louis's. His name is Al. Excuse me sir, I forgot your last name," Mr. Edwards said apologetically.

"Al is good," the man said. Faith just nodded her head toward Al. That is as much acknowledgment as she wanted to give this man. He made the hairs on the back of her neck stand up.

Faith got chills as she felt a hand slide around her waist from behind. She knew instantly who it was. "Cousin Louis how are you?" she said without even turning around.

"Why cousin Faith, however, did you know that it was me?" he asked with a sheepish grin.

"Oh, I could smell you," she hissed.

Louis laughed it off and said, "I will take that, no matter how you meant it," he winked as he walked off.

Faith turned as she heard a fork dinging against a wine glass. It was her father.

"Attention. Let's all go to the dining room so that we can start dinner," Mr. Edwards said as he turned to walk, and everyone followed him.

The food smelled divine. There was a ham in the middle of the twelve-foot-long table with chairs on both sides. Her father took his place at the head of the table as Cousin Louis took his place at the other end. Faith chose the seat to the right of her father. Everyone else gathered around and began to eat. Conversation was light and during the desert course everything was going off without a hitch.

Faith heard a moan to her left and saw her father as he began to fall over. Faith jumped up! "Papa! Papa! Someone please help me! Papa!" The room began to spin around her.

The doctor walked from Mr. Edwards's room and looked at Faith. "Ms. Edwards, he needs rest. This does not look good. He had some sort of attack. I am not sure what this is, but he needs rest. His pulse is erratic, and his breathing labored. I left tonic by the bed to help east his stress."

"Thank you. Can I go in to see him?" Faith asked.

"Yes, but keep all visits short and no stress," the doctor replied.

Faith turned around and entered her father's room. He looked frailer than Faith had ever seen him. She sat beside the bed and held his hands in her hands. She blinked back tears. She felt so alone. Her father is the only family she has left. Well, except Cousin Louis. That thought made Faith shudder. She felt her father squeeze her hand.

"Father, you scared me," she whispered.

He reached out and touched her face. "Faith, I am sorry. I have not been feeling well and was trying to push through it and not concern you."

Faith placed her hand on top of his on her cheek. "Papa, I am not a baby anymore. You cannot protect me from everything."

"I know. We need to have a talk." He tried to sit up.

"Papa, we can talk later. You rest now," she patted his hand.

"No, I need to talk to you. We need to find you a husband. I do not know how much time I have left here, and I do not want to leave you being unwed. It is too dangerous. I need to know that you are taken care of and protected," he said sadly.

"Papa, I can take care of myself. I do not need to be married. If I ever marry, it will be out of love, not necessity," Faith tilted her head stubbornly.

"Faith, I wish it were that simple," he shook his head.

"It is that simple," Faith said quietly, defiant.

"We will discuss this later. I need to rest."

"Yes Papa, please rest," she left the room silently.

Faith shut the door quietly and leaned against it. She thought. "What was making Papa feel so bad? Why is he suddenly not feeling good? This made no sense. He has always been healthy. He is forty-five years old and still young and healthy."

Faith walked somberly down the stairs and bid the guests good night. Only Cousin Louis remained.

"How is old Uncle doing?" Louis asked.

"He is resting."

"Sure, seemed odd for him to get sick all of a sudden, didn't it?" he drawled.

"He will be fine. He is tired," Faith said, but could feel her hairs prickling at the base of her neck.

"Good night, Louis. Have a safe trip riding back into town."

"I believe I will tether my horse here tonight, Faith. I have business to address with Uncle when he is feeling up to it."

"He will not be up to that for a couple of days," with saying that Faith left him standing in the parlor.

Chapter 2
Vayne

Vayne Lafitte was riding with a purpose. His black stallion was sensing his urgency as he lunged forward. Vayne took one glimpse over his shoulder and could see his ship docked in the cove, hidden from sight. His dark hair curled at the nape of his neck. Beads of sweat dripped down his neck into his shirt. He knew that he needed to keep a low profile as he headed into town to get supplies, trying to go undetected, and not cause a stir. As he was passing by a creek something caught his eye. He slowed down his stallion, so as not to disturb this beautiful creature. Her hair was fire red, and she was laying in the grass humming to herself. She looked to be twenty. She was small in stature. He smiled to himself as he watched her. He raised one dark eyebrow as he heard her groan and could tell she was not happy with wherever she was going. He backed up easily and went on his way. He did not know why, but he felt like he had known her forever. He shook his head and got back on task.

As he neared town he slowed down, to not draw attention to himself. The last thing he needed was attention. He needed to keep a low profile. He had been expelled from Texas and he did not need to be expelled from Mississippi too. Some did not understand his agenda. Considered a criminal by some and a hero by others, he just wanted to get supplies, get back to the ship, get back to his little island of paradise, and stay secluded. He came to a slower pace as he reached town. He could see Edwards Banking at the end of the street, standing huge, like a crown marking the head of a king. To each side of the road were little shops, a saloon, and a bookstore. He knew the owner of the bookstore. He would have to get back soon and visit with Ms. Alma. Ms. Alma knew Vayne. She has known him since he was a small boy. She was a friend of his mama's. He made a mental note to stop in and see her.

He walked into Edwards Bank nonchalantly to make a deposit. The bank was the biggest building in town. As you walk into the bank, you see six windows with tellers in the front and to the left is an office door. As he was walking in, he heard raised voices coming from the office. He saw a round; grisly looking man walk out smoking a cigar and another younger man with red hair walk out. There was hostility going on between the three gents. He noticed the man at the desk in the office looked distraught and upset.

As Vayne walked out of the bank, he heard someone yell his name. He froze for a split second, then glanced over his shoulder and smiled. It was his friend, Trent. Trent was medium height, slight build with blonde hair and blue eyes. He was breathing hard as he walked up.

"Man, I thought that was you! It has been a long time! How you been?" Trent grinned.

"I am good. I was trying to keep a low profile. I did not know you were back in these parts," Vayne kept walking.

"Oh yes, got into town a while back. Nothing feels as good as being back home, does it?" Trent said.

"No, it doesn't, but I got to get back. It was nice seeing you again, we need to catch up soon," Vayne said as he was walking away. He hated to ignore his friend, but he had to get to stepping, he might have drawn attention to himself.

Trent, not phased, kept walking with him. "Vayne, what is going on, you're acting like you don't know me."

Vayne glanced over and said, "We can catch up later."

Trent stopped walking and just shrugged, "Look me up when you get back in town."

As Vayne made his way back to his horse, he remembered he needed to see Ms. Alma, but he knew today was not the time to do that. He had not even gotten supplies yet, and it looked like he may need to come back later to do that, since he saw his friend Trent in town.

As he neared the ship, he glanced around and got a feeling someone was near him. He could not place where, though. As he neared the ship, he could see the sails of the Lady Ebony blowing in the wind. He smiled to himself and said, "I'm back, ole girl."

All his men, what few he had left, were bustling around on the dock, cleaning, and scrubbing, and getting the bounty where it needed to be stored. The deckhand, Paddy, walks up, "Sir, we got stuff below deck and stashed away. We got quite a bit this time. When will we make the drop?"

"We will get it to the people as soon as I am sure we have enough. We got non-perishables, so time should not be a problem this time," he stuck his hands into his pockets.

"Aye, aye, sir," Paddy grinned his toothless grin, and Vayne could not help but smile. He respected his men as they respected him.

"Paddy?" Vayne called his name.

"Sir?"

"Make sure you get you something to eat and take something extra for your wife and kids," Vayne said as he was walking away.

"Aye," Paddy responded.

As Vayne walked below deck to his quarters, he could not help but think about the red headed, green-eyed beauty he had seen earlier. He wondered what her story was. Who was she and would he ever see her again. He was thinking of her as he drifted off to sleep with the rocking of the ship.

Chapter 3
The Proposal

Faith woke up startled. She needed to go and check on Papa and see how he was doing. She lit the candle and opened her bedroom door. As she walked toward his door, she noticed it was ajar. She could see a faint glow coming from the room and shadows walking around.

Who is in the room with Papa? She thought.

As she was about the walk into the room, a hand reached out and kept her from squealing. It was Maw Sally. "Do not go in there, child. Shhhhhh, I am going to move my hand, but you got to be quiet as a mouse."

Faith whispered, "What is going on?"

Maw Sally stated, "I do not know, but what I do know is you, me, and your Papa are the only ones supposed to be here and we are both out here. So I know whoever is in there don't need to be."

Faith's eyes went wild, "I must go to Papa! I cannot just stand here and not do anything!"

Faith broke loose from Maw Sally's grasp and ran to the door. As she got to the door, Cousin Louis met her.

"What are you doing in my father's room?" Faith demanded.

"I was checking on him to see how he is doing," Louis smirked.

"Who else is in there? Why are you at the plantation at this hour?"

"We had some business to deal with and figured we would kill two birds with one stone, so to speak," he said.

"Move out of my way, Louis. I want to see my father," Faith tried to push past him.

As Faith was trying to push past, a short, grizzly looking person walked out of the door. Faith recognized him from the dinner party. His name was Al. He tipped his hat as he walked by Faith, with a cigar clenched between his teeth. Faith pushed past them into her father's room.

"Papa, are you okay?" she asked as she rushed to his bedside.

"I am fine Faith."

"What is going on?" she pushed and had that look in her face that shows she will not give up if not answered.

"Faith, there are things going on at the bank right now. Louis and Dexter came to see me today with that Al Brute. Louis is up to no good."

Faith leaned toward her father, "What do you mean no good?"

"I mean, he has somehow gotten Edwards Plantation and Edwards Banking's ownership over into his name. I do not know how he did it. I never signed any paperwork, but he has it and everything is now his."

Faith felt her face flush. "Why that low down, no good.... ."

John Edwards grabbed his daughter's hand with a force that startled her. "Faith, you listen to me. What I am about to tell you, you will have to do what I say. Do you understand?"

"Yes Papa."

"When the time comes and if something happens to me, you must leave. You must leave Edwards Plantation and get far away. Do you understand?" He looked at her as if begging her to understand.

"I refuse to leave my home. You need to tell me why. Why must I leave my home and everything that I know?"

"Faith, Louis has the bank and plantation in his name, however, your name is still attached. The only way he will ever get full control of anything is if marries you. He has asked for your hand in marriage." he stated.

"What! He is my cousin. I will never marry him. Never!"

"Faith, if something happens to me, you need to run. Do you understand?"

"Yes Papa, but not without a fight."

John Edwards could not help but be a proud Papa in that moment, but he was also terrified. He was terrified of what would become of Faith if something happened to him. He needed to know she was safe until he could get this figured out.

"Faith, you run on along to bed. I will take you to town to work at the bookstore in the morning. I will stay in town until you're done and bring you back home," he was trying to sound stronger than he felt.

"Yes Papa," Faith left and went to her room. She felt like she had a dark cloud over her, and she could not put all the pieces together of what was going on.

As Faith walked out, John Edwards took a long deep breath. *How did this happen?* He thought. *How could Louis have done this right under my nose?* He thought that when he came to the bank two days ago, it was a joke. He thought that someone was trying to play a fast one on him. He was having a challenging time understanding and figuring out how he could fix this. His sweet sister, God rest her soul, would be so disappointed in how her only son had turned out. He knew that Louis could have questionable character, but this completely came as a shock. To think he asked to marry his Faith. He knew he would never willingly let him marry her, but he had to find a way to protect Faith and keep her safe. He would figure this out if it were the last thing he did. Louis would not get away with this.

Maw Sally stayed in the hallway for a long while. Then she went to her room to pray. She prayed for her sweet Faith, she prayed for Mr. Edwards. They had always been so good to her, and she knew that something was awry. She could feel it down deep in her bones. She knew that she would have to intervene somehow. She knew that she would do whatever it takes to keep her family safe. This was the only family she had left. Her husband, daughter, and grandson had died years earlier. They had met Mr. Edwards and Mrs. Edwards briefly. Maw Sally winced as she thought; *Sweet Mrs. Edwards would roll over in her grave if she could see what this Louis bastard was trying to do.* Maw Sally leaned back in her rocker and closed her eyes. She knew that the time would come when she would be able to help them as much as they have helped her.

Chapter 4
Let's Go Home

Louis Edwards knew that he was no looker. However, he knew what he wanted. He wanted it all. He wanted Edwards Plantation, Edwards Banking and finally, yet most importantly, he wanted Faith Edwards. He knew the age difference but did not care. He had wanted her since she was a kid. He knew it was not right. He did not care. He was tired of being seen as second best. John Edwards had it all. His mother was left with the scraps after John inherited it all. Yes, John may have been the eldest and his mother taken care of, but Louis felt like he deserved more. He would have it.

As he walked out of the house after speaking with Faith, he knew it was only a matter of time before his plan would fall into place. He had asked John for his blessing to marry her. John looked at him with disgust. Like Faith was too good for him. In his mind he knew he had John right where he wanted him. Let him marry Faith and at least keep his job at the bank, or do not let him marry Faith and lose it all. He was hoping the threats from tonight would put the wheel into motion. Faith set his insides on fire. It was a lust that he knew was wrong, but he also could not control. He knew what he needed to ease his thirst tonight. He would go into town and see his favorite saloon girl. Daisy always knew how to make him feel better, even when she did not want to.

He walked into the saloon and looked around. He did not see Daisy. He headed toward the bar.

"Where is Daisy?" He asked the bartender as he ordered a whiskey, straight up.

The bartender flicked his head toward the upstairs, "She has a suitor."

"Damn, guess I will have to wait."

Daisy was upstairs with her favorite customer, Trent. He was so tender and easy with her. He did not like her doing this job, but understood it was only temporary until she could get on her feet and established. Daisy was a voluptuous, vivacious woman. She had thick blonde hair, round breasts, sky blue eyes, and a dimple in her left cheek. She was childlike in her smile and demeanor. She came from a poor background and wanted a different life. This is not what she intended but it is what she got.

Daisy was resting her head on Trent's chest, "Let me take you away from this Daisy. You are too good to be doing this type of work. You know that I love you and would provide for you. I do not like the thought of you with other men."

Daisy smiled and rolled over and rested her chin on his chest and looked up at him, "Now Trent. You would be tired of me in a week. Then where would I be? I would be out on my own again and must start over."

Trent shook his head and just could not understand why Daisy found it so hard to see that he loved her. He had loved her from the first time he paid for her services. Since then, he has not paid one time. He would gladly pay, but she will not accept it from him because they have a personal relationship and not a business one. "Daisy, dammit, let me love you."

"Trent, if we are meant to be, it will happen. We do not have to be in a hurry."

"Daisy, it been two years since we first met. How much longer do you want to keep doing this?"

"Until I save enough money to know I can stand on my own two feet and we both can get the hell out of this town."

He reached down, kissed her, and said, "Well, how about you show me how good I got it right now and I may just drop it tonight."

"Why yes sir, I think I can manage that," she rolled over on top of him and he moaned.

"Yes ma'am, I can drop it for tonight."

Trent walked down the stairs after leaving Daisy, walked to the bar, and ordered a whiskey. Leaning on one elbow, the man beside him nodded and got up and went toward the stairs. Louis walked slowly up the stairs towards Daisy's boudoir. Just as he was about the knock, she opened the door.

"Louis, you startled me," she said exasperated.

"I need to see you tonight to help me get my mind off of some things."

Daisy smiled, "Louis, not tonight, I just had my last customer, and I was fixing to go get freshened up."

Louis's eyes grew dark, "I am not asking you Daisy. I am telling you. I am a paying customer, and you will serve me."

"No, I will not Louis. You are drunk and you need to leave. Now," Daisy backed away and tried to shut the door.

Louis was too fast for her. He grabbed the door, forced his way in, and locked the door behind him. "Daisy, you will serve me. You whore, you do what I say." As Louis said this, Daisy bolted for the door. He grabbed her long, blonde hair and with a jerk, she was her back on the floor. Pain shot through her body from head to toe and the wind was knocked out of her.

"Louis please stop!"

Before she could get the words out, his hands were around her throat, and he was on top of her. She could not scream. Pure terror coursed through her. Her legs kicked but she could not get his hands from around her throat so that she could breathe. Louis picked her up by the throat and threw her on the bed. He was on top of her in seconds. He ripped her gown open and exposed her breasts. His mouth went down on one breast, and she was clawing at him trying to make him stop. He slapped her hard across the face she felt her teeth rattle and she could taste the metallic blood in her mouth. He loosened on her throat, and she gasped for air.

"Get off of me!" she screamed.

"I will have you Faith," he said through gritted teeth.

"I am not Faith. I am Daisy. Who is Faith?" she said through clenched teeth.

She understood something clearly at last come back into his eyes at this question and he released her. Louis looked at her confused. He got up from the bed, walked over to the water pitcher, and washed his face. He took her a rag and handed it to her to clean herself up. She dabbed at her mouth. She could feel her lip swollen and bruised. She walked over to the dressing mirror and winced when she saw her face. At this moment, she knew. She was done with this line of work. Trent was right. She deserved better. She deserved him.

Daisy asked him to leave again and this time he did. He did not look at her. He did not apologize. He tiptoed out and shut the door. She packed her bags and knew as she looked around, she never wanted to come back to this place again. She walked down the stairs with a blank stare. She arrived at the bottom of the stairs and Trent looked up from the bar. She had forgot what a mess she looked.

Trent looked up from the bar and his smiled faded. He could feel rage as he saw her face and the look in her eyes. He walked slowly toward her and did not know how to respond. He reached up and ran his thumb over her lips and her bruised eye. He bent down and kissed her tenderly. She looked up at him.

"Trent please take me away from here. You were right. I deserve better. I deserve to be with you and for us to be happy. Please just take me away," she cried into his shoulder as she grabbed him and held on.

Trent picked her up, carried her from the saloon, and said, "Let's go home, Daisy."

Chapter 5
The Meeting

Faith was up early the next morning. She slept little the night before. Her mind was racing with a million different thoughts. She put on her simple blue cotton dress with a small petticoat and her riding boots.

Father might take me into town, but I can ride by myself.

"Are you ready to go to the bookstore?" John stated as he looked up from his breakfast.

"Yes, but I am going to ride alongside of you on my steed."

"Okay. We need to get going," he said standing up.

On the way into town, Faith's mind was still thinking about last night. *What is Louis up to?* It was a beautiful fall day. There was a cool breeze blowing, and she loved feeling the sun on her face. As they drew nearer to town, she spotted the bookstore and Ms. Alma unlocking the door.

"Good morning Ms. Alma," Faith said as cheerfully as she could.

"Well, hello there Miss Faith. I am glad to see you made it today. I got a few things you might be interested in."

"Oh Ms. Alma, I came to help you today and volunteer in the store. I know the last time you had some things you needed cataloged, and I wanted to help you get that sorted and taken care of."

Ms. Alma smiled her big smile. She was a chubby woman, in her mid-sixties, with a bubbly personality. "Faith you are a darling. I appreciate that."

Faith and Ms. Alma walked into the store chatting.

John Edwards made his way to the bank. He needed to go into his office and look into the paperwork that Louis had showed him. How he got a set of paperwork with everything changed and dated right after the originals was a shock to him. He had a deed, a bill of sale, and documents for the bank. They were forged, but how would he be able to prove this. He felt as if there was no way out. If he could just get those papers that Louis had and destroy them, this entire thing would be over. The first thing he wanted to do was to go to the bank, get his original paperwork, and make sure it was safe. He must have the originals. John made it over to the bank. He went into his office. He moved the rug and opened the safe. The papers were there. He would make sure to put these papers where no one would think to look for them. He knew just the place.

Vayne was headed back into town. Hopefully, t*his time he will not see anyone he knew. Especially this early.* As Vayne headed into town, he remembered he wanted to go by and see Ms. Alma at the bookstore. He had not seen the ole songbird in quite some time and he knew he would get a scolding when he did. He smiled to himself. *She was the closest thing to the family he had left in this world. He needed to make it a point to drop in more often.*

Vayne tethered his horse and opened the door to the bookstore. The little bell jingled as he let the door close.

Faith looked up from the counter, "Can I help you?"

Vayne felt like hot water hit him in the face. That red hair, those green eyes, those full lips. *This is the girl I saw by the creek,* he swallowed hard. "Is Ms. Alma here?"

Faith smiled, "She is. I will fetch her for you."

As Faith walked around the counter to go to the back of the store to get Ms. Alma, his eyes followed every curve of her and took it in. He felt his heart skip. *I usually have more control than this. What is wrong with me?*

"Well, I will be! Vayne Lafitte!" Alma squealed and ran up to him and gave him a motherly hug. "Just where have you been young man? I have missed you," she said wagging her finger.

"I have been busy, but I am going to try to come by more often to check on you."

"How rude of me. This is Faith Edwards. She comes in from time to time and volunteers to help at times. You know, since my sweet Vayne is not around enough to help," she teased.

Faith smiled and held out her hand. Vayne felt like a school kid and got shy but made himself reach out and touch her hand. He felt like he had moths flapping around inside his chest. His heart was pounding. He was feeling frustrated with himself.

"Nice to meet you. Are you from around here? I have never seen you before?" she asked.

"You could say I am from here and many other places too."

"Where?" Faith squinted her eyes.

The question took Vayne by surprise, "Well, I have traveled a lot. I, um, I have a boat."

"Really? A boat? Where do you keep your horse when you are on a small boat and travel? I saw you have a horse outside?" Faith tilted her head.

Vayne thought, *she is a curious little thing*.

Ms. Alma was watching the two, amused. She could hardly contain herself. She knew exactly who and what Vayne was. "A boat," She thought and chuckled to herself. "A boat my foot."

"Ms. Alma, I am going to get going. I have some things to do in town today. I will see you soon," he headed to the door.

Faith looked up at this man. He was handsome, tall, and strong with broad shoulders and strong hands. She almost did not want him to leave. She did not understand why because she had only just met him. Before he made it to the door, Faith said, "Vayne? It was nice meeting you. I will be here tomorrow if you would like to drop by again. I mean I can use the help and I know that Ms. Alma would love it. If you want to that is."

Vayne smiled to himself. This little woman might be interested in him. He looked at her and smiled, "I might just do that Ms. Faith," he tilted his hat and walked out the door.

Vayne was crossing over to the Saloon when he saw Trent headed in his direction. Trent had a serious expression on his face. He knew Trent well enough to know that something was wrong.

"Hey Trent, want to grab a drink?" Vayne asked.

Trent said, "Oh we are friends again now since you didn't know me the last time you saw me."

Vayne tilted his head, "You know what that was about. I told you. What is going on?"

"My girl Daisy got attacked and I am looking to find the man who did it," Trent said as he downed a shot.

"Who would want to hurt Daisy?"

"She will not tell me. She said it was not worth it. She left the Saloon. She left the night it happened. She is out at my place, well mine and her place."

Vayne knew well enough that this must have been a violent attack for Daisy to leave the profession. Trent had been begging her for a long while now. "Is she okay? She hurt badly?"

Trent took a breath, "He roughed her up fairly good. She is being quiet right now. I can tell she is upset. She will not talk about it. She said leave it alone."

Vayne just shook his head. "It will all come out in the wash eventually and he will get what's coming to him."

Trent took in a breath, "Yes, you are right. I just want to give to him what he gave to her."

Vayne shook his head, downed his shot. "C'mon, let's get out of here. I got something I want to show you."

They both headed out of town, toward the *Lady Ebony*. As they neared the ship, Trent saw the sails in the distance. "I see you got her up and running again."

"Yep, took me a year, but I got her put back together and got my crew back," Vayne said squinting his eyes in the sun.

"Vayne, where have you been?"

"I got expelled from Texas because they didn't believe in what I was doing. So, I had to lay low for a while and thought what better place to go than back home, where no one would expect me to go."

"I get what you are doing. Playing Robin Hood and taking from the rich to give to the poor."

"No, I steal from criminals and give to the less fortunate. There is a big difference." Vayne said pointedly. "Seeing what I have in this world and the crooks getting rich, while others are starving, I feel like I have to do something. When I think about my mother and what she went through, I must do something to make her proud and honor her memory."

Vayne looked off into the distance, lost in memories, "I understand Vayne. You need to make your own family and make your mother proud. Let her legacy live on through you and your children," Trent said thoughtfully.

Vayne understood what Trent was saying. He just felt an obligation to keep fighting this fight until something or someone showed him a different path.

"She is a beauty!" Trent said, admiring The Lady Ebony.

The Lady Ebony was made of beautiful, polished mahogany. The rigging was meticulously ran from the sails, masts, and booms. The mast above the deck of the ship was massive. The sail was beautifully made with an Ebony stone, which represented Vayne's mother. It signified her Native American heritage. The bow, beautifully carved in the Native American symbol of the wolf. The ship also had cannons surrounding all sides.

"I am proud of her. I think my mother would be very proud too. It is her namesake, The Lady Ebony."

Trent knew that it was important to Vayne to keep his mother's legacy and memory alive. He knew that what Vayne really needed was a family. To keep the legacy alive and to learn whom his grandmother was.

"Do you have a lot of cargo on board right now?" Trent questioned.

"Yes. Waiting on the right time to take it to where it needs to go. I passed some islands off the coast that were poor and in need. I am going to take them there when the coast is clear, and things calm down."

"Well old friend. We have made quite the journey from where we used to be. I was poor on the farm working someone else's land and you were with your mother on a reservation, starving. Look at us now. I work my own land and you have the beginnings of a fleet, feeding the starving."

Vayne chuckled, "That we have my old friend. That we have."

Chapter 6
Book Store Date

Faith was up extra early to head to the bookstore. She was not sure why, but she just had a feeling it was going to be a great day. She rushed to get dressed, ran downstairs, grabbed an apple, pecked Maw Sally on the cheek, and was out the door, into the barn, on the horse and down the road.

Vayne was up early and headed into town, when he saw Faith racing across the field headed toward town. He caught up to her and whistled. She saw him and slowed down to a trot.

"Where are you off to in such a hurry this morning?"

"Oh, I am just out for a ride. Thought I may go to the bookstore today. Not sure yet," she said.

"It is a nice day to just mosey and talk. Don't you think?" Vayne asked with a raised brow.

Faith smiled and was surprised when her heart did a little jump, "Yes, a nice mosey would be fun."

Vayne could barely hide his smile as he watched her. He did not know why he was so intrigued with this young woman. She was beautiful, but he had been around beautiful women before. He just genuinely liked her. That was a rare find in his world.

"Where are you coming from?" Faith asked.

"I am, um, coming from my boat."

"I need to see this boat that you speak of. Is it big?"

"You could say it is a good size," he smiled.

"What do you do for a living? Do you fish?"

"Not exactly. I guess you could say I help people."

"Help people how? What do you do?" Faith asked again.

Vayne did not mind her questions. In fact, he thought it was adorable how she just said what was on her mind. "Well, enough about me, I can explain more about that later," he said changing the subject.

"I volunteer at the bookstore and help Ms. Alma. I work around the plantation and help when that is needed. Which is not a lot these days. Things have slowed down. My father owns the bank in town, well, used to own the bank."

Vayne raised an eyebrow, "What do you mean, used to own? That seems like an odd thing to say?"

"Well, there is some stuff going on. I would rather not talk about right now," she shifted in her saddle.

Vayne thought, *she changed the subject truthfully and to the point. I like that.*

"Where do you live Ms. Faith?"

"I live on Edwards Plantation back up the road a ways."

"I know Edwards Plantation. My mother took me there once when I was a child." Vayne looked away into the distance lost in thought.

"Your mother brought you to Edwards Plantation?" Faith was genuinely surprised.

"Yes. We went to the plantation on one cold Christmas Day. There was no food on the reservation. We were half starved. My grandmother worked for Edwards Plantation and we went there to see if we could get food and they were good to us and fed us and kept us warm. Our tribe moved on, but my mother stayed here.

"Wait. Your grandmother worked at Edwards Plantation?' Faith was astonished.

"Yes. That was a long time ago. I was just a lad and barely remember it. Nevertheless, I do remember that we felt safe and warm. Let us get moving. Ms. Alma will give me a scolding if you are much later to the bookstore," he said picking up his pace.

Faith could not believe what she was hearing. *Who was his grandmother? Who was his mother? How is this possible?*

Faith and Vayne rode in silence the rest of the way to the bookstore. Each lost in their thoughts. They both walked inside together to see Ms. Alma. She was bustling around the back of the store. She heard the bell when they came in.

"Hello, can I help you? I will be with you in a minute," they heard her call from the back of the store.

"It's just us Ms. Alma."

"Oh hello! I did not realize you were coming to the store today," she said breathing heavy trying to lift a box from the top shelf. Vayne reached up, took it from her, and sat it on the table.

"What can we help you do Ms. Alma? We are here and we might as well be useful?" Faith said as she watched Vayne out of the corner of her eye. She secretly wanted to spend more time with him. She wanted to know more about him. She was intrigued.

"I tell you what, I need some errands ran. You think you two can manage that?"

Vayne cringed. He was trying to keep to himself. However, he obliged. Faith and Vayne set out in town to do Ms. Alma's errands. They walked and talked while they were in town.

Faith was lost in conversation when she felt a hand come around her waist and she froze. Vayne could tell by her face that this was not a welcomed touch.

Without even turning around, she said "Hello cousin Louis."

"Cousin Faith how you always know it's me?" he asked.

"I will tell you the same thing I always tell you Cousin Louis. I smelled you," she gritted through her teeth.

Vayne felt heat rising to his face. Faith saw his jaw tighten. Vayne held out his hand to shake hands.

"What is your name again? Louis?" Vayne asked with a fake smile.

"Louis. Louis Edwards," he answered. They shook hands. Vayne had a tight grip on Louis's hand and began to squeeze. He leaned in and said, "It's nice to meet you. Now, let me tell you a secret. Women do not like being touched without their consent. So, I suggest you think about that the next time you want to touch Ms. Faith again."

Louis's face drained of all color and the pain in his hand kept him from speaking. He just nodded.

Faith turned around and smiled, "See you around Cousin Louis."

Vayne put his arm around Faith's waist and led her away from Louis. He glanced over at her, "Are you okay?"

Faith said, "Me? Oh, yes. I am fine. Sometimes I do not know whether he is dangerous, crazy or both."

Vayne did not like the sound of that, and he did not like the way he looked at Faith. He could sense he was a very sinister and dangerous man. Vayne would keep an eye on Louis. They finished their errands and headed back to the shop. Alma was getting ready to close when they got back. They bid her goodbyes.

Vayne looked at Faith, "I am going to ride with you home and see you to your door safely."

Faith wanted to protest, but she honestly was not ready to leave him yet. So, she agreed.

They talked on the way back to Edwards Plantation. As they rode onto the property, Vayne noticed how massive the house was. It was a white plantation home. Adorned with eight columns on the front porch, which wound all the way around the house. In the front of the house was a huge pecan orchard. To the right side was a field and the creek, where he saw her standing, ran along the side. To the left of the house was a chicken coop, and butcher house. The back of the house, toward the back of the property, had a huge barn with horses. It was a spectacular site.

They slowed their pace and came down the long dirt drive and both could feel they were not quite ready to let the day end yet. Dismounted their horses, tethered them, and walked up to the front door.

Faith smiled shyly and said, "Do you want to sit and talk a while more on the porch?"

"I would like that very much. I mean, if you are up for it," he smiled.

They made their way to the huge swing at the end of the porch on the left. They both sat down and just swung in silence for a few minutes. Faith leaned her head back, let her hair fall over the back of the swing, and closed her eyes. Vayne watched her.

She finally spoke, "Do you ever just want to be?"

Vayne tilted his head intently, "What do you mean?"

"I mean to just be happy and not worry and feel like everyone tells you what you should and should not do?" She still had her head tilted back with her eyes closed.

"I understand what you mean. You feel like you do what everyone else wants, but you either are not able to do what you want, or you have lost yourself and do not know what you want," he said, as he leaned his head back and closed his eyes.

Faith was taken aback because he understood what she meant. She smiled to herself, "I had a really nice time today."

"I did too, Ms. Faith," he said.

"Please just call me Faith. I hate people calling me Ms. Especially my friends."

"Is that what we are? Friends?" Vayne asked smiling.

"Yes. We are friends. I want to keep being friends. I want to keep seeing each other and talking. I feel comfortable with you," she said.

Vayne knew that Faith was being honest in her words. He felt like she was wise beyond her years. He knew in his heart that he was in this for more than friendship, but he would have to let her discover that on her own. She would realize it in her own time. Until that time, he would be the best friend she ever had.

Chapter 7
Raging

Louis Edwards was furious. *How dare this man insult him and humiliate him like that! Faith thought it was funny too. He saw her smirk and makes fun of him. She would pay for that mistake and never make it again.*

"I will make sure that she knows she will respect me. I will break her spirit and she will follow my every command. She will understand that disrespect will not be tolerated. She will learn her lesson," he raged, while speaking aloud to himself.

He removed the ice pack from his hand, put his jacket back on, and left to head over to Saloon to have a drink and get some relief from one of the Saloon girls. When he opened the door, Al was waiting outside for him. "What do you want Al? I am busy."

Al lit his cigar and placed it between his yellow teeth, "I got some news for you that you might be interested in."

"What news?" Louis stopped and raised a brow.

"Dexter Scott went into the safe to get the original paperwork for Edwards Plantation and Edwards Banking," Al said and then took a puff of the cigar.

Fanning the smoke from his face, Louis said, "And what? Did he get it?"

"No. It was gone," Al took another drag off the cigar.

"Gone? Did he look under the rug behind the desk in the floor?"

"Yes. That is the one."

"And the papers were not there?" Louis asked.

"No," Al said taking another drag.

"We must get those papers, or we are all out! You will not have a cut of anything, Dexter is out, and I am out! Those papers must be destroyed!" Louis spewed.

"We could always burn down Edwards Plantation. They are more than likely hid there," Al stated.

"Burn Edwards Plantation! Burn the one thing that I have wanted? Burn the entire reason this plan is at work! You have to be out of your mind!"

"Careful how you speak to me rich boy," Al whispered.

"Go do your job. Find the paperwork. Do whatever it is you have to do to find the paperwork. If the paperwork is not found, then this all falls apart. We will be looking at the end of a noose," Louis blasted.

Al walked off slowly, puffing on his cigar. He reminded Louis of a nasty slug and he cringed.

At least he will do what needs to be done. He has the stomach for it, Louis thought.

Al walked across the street to Edwards Banking. He walked in and asked, "I need to speak to Dexter Scott."

Dexter walks out, his eyes big, "What are you doing here?"

Al looked at him blankly and said, "Where are the papers?"

"I told you. They were not in the safe when I checked."

"Are you sure about that? I think you are lying and have double crossed us," Al puffed his cigar.

"Of course, I am sure. What would I have to gain by lying to you?" he asked.

"You might not have anything to gain by lying but you have a lot to lose if you are."

"Look, I did my part. The paperwork was not there. So please leave me alone."

Al turned and walked out of the bank. He figured that Dexter was telling the truth, but he wanted to have a little fun with him.

Al left the bank, turned right, and headed out of town. He decided it better take a closer look at Edwards Plantation. He mounted his horse and took off out of town. He found a spot on a hill, in front of the plantation on the other side of the pecan orchard with a beautiful view of the front of the house. This would be his perch for a while so that he could stalk his prey and see what they were doing. He chugged a bottle of whiskey, smoked his cigar, and was enjoying his view when something caught his eye on the porch. He smiled to himself when he saw them, because he knew how this would make Louis feel. He chuckled and said aloud, "This should be good."

Chapter 8
Home

Daisy was stirring the pot on the wood burning stove when she heard Trent open the cabin door. She smiled as she turned around to greet him. She never thought she could be as happy as she was in this little cabin in the woods. It was her safe place.

"I am glad you are home. Supper will be ready in a few. Get washed up and I will set you a place."

Trent smiled, "Yes ma'am. It sure smells good, whatever that is."

"It is lentil soup. It is about the only thing I know how to cook. You will have to teach me to cook. I know you thought you were getting a domesticated woman, but I am afraid you were wrong," Daisy said as she spooned the soup into his bowl.

"You are perfect just the way you are. I can teach you all sorts of stuff," he winked.

She poured herself a bowl and sat across from him at the wooden table that he had made. The cabin was modest with the necessities and that was simply fine with her. Trent was looking at her and noticed the bruises were starting to turn darker. It made his stomach tighten just looking at her face.

"How are you feeling today?" he asked.

"I am good," she glanced away.

That glance did not go unnoticed by Trent. He knew she still had some healing to do on the inside before she would feel better. "Well, I saw my friend Vayne in town earlier. You will meet him soon. He is an upstanding person. I am hoping he will settle down soon. We go way back. We knew each other as kids and did some work together and had some plans," he said as he spooned soup into his mouth.

"What kind of plans did you boys have?"

"We had plans to start a ranch together and maybe open it up to folks who want to work and help others. He is all about helping the less fortunate. He has this notion that helping others will somehow keep his mother's legacy alive. My thought is to keep her legacy alive he needs to get himself a nice woman, have a couple kids, and be happy. That is what she would have wanted," Trent drank the rest of his soup from the bowl.

Daisy smiled, "Seems to me doing both might be twice as good. He could settle down, have a couple kids, and help the less fortunate."

"You are one smart woman. Domesticated or not."

Daisy got up, cleared the table, and poured them both a cup of coffee. She handed him his cup and smiled, "Drink up! You are going to need your energy for later."

"Later? What is later?" Trent questioned.

"You will find out. I mean if you be nice and all," she smirked.

"Oh I see. You going to get me spoiled with all this when the new wears off," he laughed.

"Nah, you forget who you talking to mister. The new will not wear off," she laughed.

"Well, why do we have to wait until later? We can handle this situation right now," he smirked.

Daisy laughed and sat down onto his lap, "I need to talk to you about something."

Trent leaned back in his chair with her on his lap. "Okay, shoot. What do you need to talk to me about?"

"I never talked to you much about things that some of my," she cleared her throat, "gentleman friends talked to me about."

"Okay. What do you mean?"

"Well, the person that hurt me. The one that attacked me the other night..." she talked very carefully because she did not want to stir up his anger again. She was not sure she would be able to stop him from tearing the man to shreds if he got his hands on him.

"Mmmhmm," he nodded.

"He liked to talk when he was drinking. Well, he said that he was planning something big. He was planning something big," she drawled.

"Daisy, would you spit it out and cut to the chase? Please ma'am?"

"Well, he said that he was going to own Edwards Plantation and Edwards Banking. I am not sure what he meant by that, but he was ranting about how John Edwards owed him and he was going to take everything, including his daughter. I never thought he had a backbone to do any of the things he talked about. That is, until he attacked me. Trent. His eyes. His eyes were empty. He is pure evil," she choked back tears.

Trent wrapped his arms around her, "If you would tell me who he is I could take care of it."

Daisy shook her head, "There is no use. It is over now. I just hope he does not do anything to anyone else. That would be a real dreadful thing. I just hope I never have to see him again. I really do."

Trent picked her up into his arms, blew out the candles, and carried her to bed. He knew that he would do everything in his power to protect her. Eventually he would find out who this yellow belly coward was and run him through.

"I love you, Daisy."

"I love you Trent," good night.

Chapter 9
Hidden

John Edwards felt relief. The original paperwork for the plantation and the bank was well hidden. Only he and one other person knew where it was. It was safe. Now to figure out how he was going to get this all managed with Louis. He was turning into a mad man. *If he thought for one second, I would let him marry Faith, he really is mad.*

He heard the front door open, and Faith walked in. He noticed something different. He watched her cross the hall with a smile. "Faith? Can you come here for a moment?"

"Yes Papa."

"How was Ms. Alma today?"

"She was good. I met a friend of hers named Vayne," she smiled and shifted on one foot.

"Vayne? Lafitte?" he asked.

"Do you know him?" she felt confused.

"I knew him as a child. I helped him and his mother years ago."

Faith pulled up a chair, "Tell me more."

"It was a time when it was freezing, and some countrymen were having a very hard time. She came here to seek refuge and assistance with her mother. It was before you were born. I never thought to discuss this with you until now. You know his grandmother very well."

"I know his grandmother?" Faith sat back in surprise.

"I never knew what became of Vayne. After him and his mother left, I never saw them again. His grandmother stayed here. Vayne was just a baby back then. He does not even remember coming here."

"Why did his grandmother stay?" she asked.

"She did not intend to stay permanently. Ebony was supposed to come back to get her but never showed up. It is as if they both vanished. We figured she went back to the village and left with her tribe. Ebony would not stay here. She felt that others needed her, and she stayed long enough for the cold to break and set out walking with Vayne. Her mother had gotten terribly ill and stayed with us until she was strong enough to travel."

"What happened to his grandmother?"

"Well, she is still here," John looked at her and leaned forward, "Faith, Maw Sally is his grandmother."

Faith flew out of the chair, "What? Wait. Maw Sally is Vayne Lafitte's grandmother?"

"There is a lot of pain behind this story. Maw Sally was devastated when she never saw them again. She knew that they must have perished or were taken, or Ebony would have come back for her. She would have never just left her here and never returned willingly."

"But Papa, he is alive. He is here. I must go tell Maw Sally at once!"

"There is more to this story. I do not have time to tell you this right now, but you cannot tell Maw Sally right now. Now is not the time. This must stay between us."

Faith shook her head, "this makes no sense at all."

"It will. I promise, but you need to keep this just between us right now. Promise me," he said.

"I promise," she was still shaking her head when she left the study and headed toward her room. Faith was still pondering when Maw Sally came into her room later in the evening.

"Chile what is going on in that pretty head of yours?" Maw Sally asked turning down her bed.

Faith swallowed, "Maw Sally, why do you not talk about your family? You never speak of them. Did you have a husband? Children?"

Maw Sally walked to the window and looked out, as if looking into the distance, remembering. "A long time ago I did. I had a man, a baby, and a grandchild," she was still looking out the window.

"Why haven't you ever spoken of them?" Faith asked.

"Sometimes things are better left unspoken if it hurt you to talk about them. Besides, I had you all these years to keep me occupied and keep my mind busy. I talked to them every night when I lay in bed. My beautiful Ebony. My Cherokee warrior princess. She was so strong willed," Maw Sally smiled through the pain.

"Will you tell me more? Please?"

"My Ebony wanted to feed the world and heal the sick. She wanted to help everyone. In the world we lived in that was not possible. In the last winter we were together, I caught ill, food was scarce, and she had a child to think about. Did I tell you I had a grandson? He was a beautiful baby. He was mischievous, for his age. Oh, he was the love of his mother's life," Maw Sally grinned.

"What about her husband? Where was he?" Faith asked.

"Maw Sally's face grew dark. There was no husband child. We were in our village when the men came through. The men came rushing in and destroying everything," Maw Sally wiped the corner of her eye.

"My man fought hard but with that many men at one time, he did not stand a chance. Men, women, and children were running everywhere when they came into our village. They were torching our furs and homes! Ebony and I were hiding in the back of the feed shed. I had my hand over her mouth to stifle her breathing. The men came into the shed. They were torching everything. The smoke started to fill the room and we could not breathe. We had to run. I made it to the door but one of the men grabbed Ebony. I tried to stop it all but I was not strong enough. He hurt her. He took advantage of sweet Ebony. Left her for dead, and with child," Maw Sally walked over to the rocker and sat down.

Faith had her hand over her mouth, "That is awful. I am so sorry," tears were streaming down Faith's face.

Maw Sally sat still for a long while. She was lost in thought, "We never spoke of what happened after that day. She would not hear of it. In her mind, her son was on this earth, because of what happened to her. She felt that it was supposed to happen. That it was a will of some type. A card she was dealt. Ebony loved her son. Her son looked just like her. Dark hair, tan skin, full lips, and brown eyes. He was a miniature replica of his mother. If only they could have made it back here. I have often wondered what he would be like, had he lived. My Ebony would have been so proud of him," Maw Sally gently rocked back and forth.

It took everything in Faith not to tell Maw Sally about Vayne. However, she knew she must keep her word to her Papa. If it were not important, he would never ask her to keep something like this a secret. Faith walked over to Maw Sally and wrapped her arms around her.

"I love you Maw Sally."

"I love you too child. You are what helped me through these years. You were my little star that shined my way."

Chapter 10
Cheerful and Ready

Vayne was in a good mood as he climbed the stairs to the deck, "Good morning, men." Each man looked at each other. This was not a normal thing on The Lady Ebony. There were groans and grunts in response as they went about their usual tasks.

"Paddy is the cargo safe and sound?"

"Aye," Paddy grunted. Paddy wondered what had his Captain in such a good mood this morning. It was out of character for him to be so cheerful. He had no clue what it was, but he liked it.

"I am going into town for a bit. I do not know when I will be back. Paddy, do you think you can keep everything in line while I am gone?"

"Aye."

"You are a man of few words Paddy," Vayne chuckled as he climbed down the plank, shaking his head.

Vayne bolted up onto his horse. He had much on his mind these days. He laughed at other men for this sort of thing and called them soft.

"You got it bad," he mumbled, talking to himself. He looked straight ahead. He had plans today He chuckled and was surprised when his heart did a little skip. He had no clue why he had these strong feelings, but he was not used to them.

As he approached Edwards Plantation, he thought about when he came here as a child. He did not remember how old he was. He just knew he was with his mother and grandmother. He had glimpses of memories and not much more. He remembered being cold and hungry and coming to this big, white house, getting warm, and his mother humming to him in his ear. He did not remember the song but just that she hummed. He remembered his grandmother bouncing him on her lap. Often, he wondered why he only remembered his mother and grandmother. He does not remember a father or anyone else. Does not remember when he went to live with Ms. Alma. He went there when he was a lad but does not remember the exact age. She took him to the country out of town. He never knew how or why. He left her home before turning sixteen years of age.

Vayne rode up to the hitching post on the side of the house. He tethered his horse and made his way to the front porch. He knocked on the door and scolded himself for feeling nervous. *What is wrong with you? You are a grown man.*

Faith opened the door and her smile explained what she did not say. "Well, hello there! Won't you come in?" she was smiling so big; it brightened her whole face. "This is a pleasant surprise."

"I wanted to come by and see if you wanted to go riding with me today? It's pretty out and the perfect weather for it."

"Sure, let me tell my father," She said, John walked out of his study, "Father, I want you to meet my friend Vayne Lafitte."

Vayne was not sure how he felt about being introduced as "my friend" It just did not feel right. He felt a closeness with her.

John held out his hand, "Vayne it is nice to meet you."

The two men shook hands and made introductions.

Faith turned to John, "Papa we are going on a ride today. I am not sure how long I will be gone. Do you need anything before I leave?"

"No, you two go and have fun and enjoy yourselves."

Faith and Vayne walked out the door, down the steps and her horse was waiting on her. The two of them walked the horses slowly, as if stalling. Vayne glanced sideways at Faith, and she was looking ahead.

"Faith, it is good to see you again."

Faith did not look his way, but answered, "It is nice seeing you again too. Can I be completely honest with you?"

"Of course, I would like for you to always be honest with me."

"I really like your company. I feel at ease with you and that says a lot. I do not normally feel at ease with men. Father of course, but not others. I have never really enjoyed their company."

Vayne smiled to himself. He liked her forwardness and honestly. She had an innocent quality about her that tugged at his heart. "I am glad to hear it. Now, can I be completely honest with you?"

She smiled, "Sure."

"I am enjoying your company too. I do not court often," he said and then caught himself.

Faith grinned, "Oh is that what we are doing? Courting?"

Vayne felt a moment of embarrassment. He did not intend on using that word. He just felt so at ease with her. It was easy to get lost in your words and just speak what was on your mind. "Yes ma'am, I guess you could say that. I want to get to know you better. I want to spend time with you. If I am being too forward, I am sorry. I just feel so at ease with you and feel…."

Faith felt the butterflies flutter against the inside of her stomach. She had never had the feeling before. Something about how he was speaking to her made her feel giddy.

"I would like to see where this goes too," she lost her words. Her feelings were all over the place at this very moment.

Vayne looked at her and smiled, "Well it is official then. We are courting. I got a friend I want you to meet. He does not live too far from here. If you are up for it, I would like to take you to their cabin."

Faith smiled, "Sounds good to me."

Vayne and Faith set off to go to Trent's Cabin. As they neared the cabin, Vayne saw Trent's horse outside and knew that they were home. He helped Faith unmounted her horse. As she slid down the front of him, he felt his stomach lurch. It was a good feeling. It was a dangerous feeling, but good, nonetheless. He wanted to hold her hand but was not sure if it was time for that yet. He knocked on the door and Trent answered.

"Yawl come on in," Vayne reached out, grabbed his friend's hand, and slapped him on the back.

"Daisy will put coffee on in the kettle. What brings you out on this fine day? It has been a while since we just sat and visited like old times. Who is this you got with you?" Trent smiled to himself.

"This is Faith. She is my," Vayne stopped himself because he honestly did not know what word to use. "Ummm she is my....."

Faith interjected, "I am his girlfriend. It is nice to meet you."

Trent had to hold back a laugh. Seeing his old friend struggle with words just touched him. Trent bowed playfully, "It is nice to meet you, Faith. This is my girl Daisy. Welcome to our little piece of paradise."

Daisy wiped her hands on her apron and crossed the room, "I am a hugger," with saying that she gave Faith and Vayne a big hug.

Faith instantly liked Daisy. She noticed her face and wondered if Trent had done that. He did not seem the type, but you never know. "So, Daisy, are you from here?"

"Not really. I came here trying to start over and ended up at the saloon. I am done with that life now. Trent took me away from that. My hero," Daisy said with a twinkle in her eye as she glanced at Trent.

Trent smiled and walked over and wrapped his arms around her from behind, "She is here with me, where she is safe."

Vayne had been watching the exchange and noticed the fading bruises on Daisy's face. He does not understand how anyone could just lay their hands on a woman. "Daisy, how are you doing?" he asked.

Daisy blushed, "I am fine."

Faith realized that there was more to the story about Daisy than she knew. They all sat in silence for a moment and watched as Daisy poured steaming cups of coffee for each of them. Vayne shifted in his chair, "So when are you two getting hitched? I mean you two been together long enough," he grinned big as he knew this would make Trent uncomfortable. To his surprise, it did not.

Trent, in one movement, hit the floor in front of Daisy, on one knee, "Daisy Mae, would you do me the honor of being my wife? I was not sure when I was going to do this, but today is just as good as any?"

Daisy squealed, "You know I will. You know I will. Yes!"

Faith grinned, and it made her heart so happy. She was not sure what to do now. "Congratulations you two," she said.

Trent looked at Vayne, "Will you be my best man? "

Vayne smiled, "You know I will."

Daisy looked around, "I do not have any friends here. I have acquaintances. Faith you are the first real person I have met here besides my doctor and Vayne here. Will you stand with me and be my matron of honor?"

Faith did not know what to say, but she knew that she could not say no, "Of course I will."

Daisy smiled and gave Faith the biggest hug. "Thank you. It will be something small. Right here at our cabin. You could help me plan some things?"

"Of course, I will. We will make it special and beautiful," Faith said, patting her hand.

They all sat around and talked for a while. Daisy realized that she had never asked Faith anything about herself. "Faith, are you from around here?"

"Oh yes. I have lived here my entire life. So has my father."

Daisy was taking a sip of her coffee, "What does your father do?"

"My Father owns Edwards Banking and Edwards Plantation," Daisy choked on her coffee.

Trent sat up forward and patted her on the back. Trent asked, "So your father owns Edwards Banking and Edwards Plantation."

"Yes. Is something wrong?" Faith asked.

Daisy and Trent looked at each other. They were not sure what to do, but they both knew that the truth was always best. "Yes, there is something that you need to know."

During this exchange, Vayne was watching, and he could tell that this was not going to be a pleasant conversation. He reached over and placed his hand on Faith's shoulder. "Go on you two. Spit it out," he said.

Trent and Daisy explained what happened to Daisy and the story about the unnamed man who hurt Daisy and how he was planning something. Faith knew exactly about whom they were talking. She said, "The man that hurt you is my cousin Louis Edwards."

Daisy brought her hand to her mouth because she did not want Trent to know who he was. She thought it better left unsaid.

Faith stated, "Louis is scum. I am trying to figure how to get my father out of this mess. I did not realize how deep his feelings went toward me. It is scary. We cannot do anything to Louis, until we figure out how to get our hands on the paperwork that he has forged for Edwards Plantation and Edwards Banking. Once we get the paperwork away from him, Trent can have his way with him. I knew that Louis was very odd, but I had no clue he had such violence in him. I have underestimated him for years."

Vayne sat and listened to this entire exchange and his stomach burned with rage. He knew, just from Daisy, what this Louis coward could do. It made him want to always keep Faith with him. This is the most time he had spent with Faith since he met her and he knew deep down whether she did, that he would go to the ends of the earth to keep her safe. He and Trent could make a plan, do some digging around, and try to figure this out. Vayne leaned over to Faith, "I think we better get going."

Faith smiled, "Yes that is best, it is getting late. We will come back soon to visit with you again," she hugged Daisy and bid her goodbyes to Trent.

As Vayne and Faith left and headed back toward Edwards Plantation, Vayne glanced over at her, 'So you are my girlfriend?" he was trying to lighten the mood.

"I don't know, you tell me. I was trying to help you out of a tight spot. You were tongue tied," she laughed.

"I feel so juvenile with this entire conversation, but yes, I think you are my girlfriend," he laughed aloud.

"Sounds good to me," Faith said.

They rode for a way and said nothing but they both knew what the other was thinking. This entire situation with Louis had to be dealt with. Faith knew that she was not safe, and that Louis was more dangerous than she ever realized.

"Faith, you need to be careful until we can get this all figured out."

"I know. I am not sure how to manage this. I must protect Papa too. He is not safe either. I did not tell you back there, but he asked for my hand in marriage from Papa in exchange for even keeping his job at the bank."

Vayne felt his face grow hot, "Well, that will not happen."

"No, it is not. I just do not know how to fix this. I do not know what to do," her voice cracked.

Vayne reached over and stopped her horse next to his. He got off his horse and helped her dismount hers. He reached down and placed his palms on each side of her face, "Faith, I need you to trust me. Do you trust me?"

"Yes. I think so. You have never given me reason not to."

"Please know that I am here with you now and you and your father are not alone. I will help you fight Louis, and he will not win," he brushed tears from the corner of her eyes with his thumbs. She looked so beautiful to him. He gently brought his face closer to hers. He kissed her forehead. His kisses went lightly over her eyes, then to her nose, he nuzzled her face in the crook of his neck, then his lips lingered over hers for a moment and brought his lips softly to hers. He felt like he was on fire at this time. He could feel her shaking against him. He knew it could not go farther than this. Not right now.

Faith felt like she had firecrackers going off inside her head. She had never been kissed. She felt his kisses on her forehead, her face, and she was anticipating how she would feel when he reached her lips. She was shaking. She felt like her entire body was alive in this very moment. She parted her lips to make way for his tongue to enter her mouth. She felt like she wanted to crawl inside him. She could not get close enough. She wrapped her arms around his neck and ran her fingers through his hair. She could feel his muscles tighten and knew that he was responding to her. She drew away breathless.

Vayne was breathing hard, "I better get you home."

"Do I have to?" she said. She saw his white teeth flash a smile.

"Yes, for now. Just for now," he laughed.

Vayne and Faith did not know it, but they were not alone. They were being watched. If they had looked up to the right, on the hill, they would have saw the flash of a cigar as Al puffed. Al smiled to himself and thought, "Louis is going to love this information. This will really cook his goose."

Chapter 11
Anger and Ebony

Louis was seething with anger at his latest report from Al. "The whore is out with this character. The one that humiliated me! John and she evidently does not understand that I am serious. They need to understand just how serious I am. It is high time that I showed them," he fumed to Al.

Al puffed on his cigar, "Do you want me to take care of the girl? I know I can make her understand just how serious you are?" Al asked smugly.

Louis's eyes changed, and he walked toward Al, "You are not to touch her. She is mine. I do not want your filthy hands on her. Do you understand?"

"Sure, whatever you say," Al said and walked out.

Louis knew that if he did not find those original papers for the bank and plantation, he would be destroyed. They needed to be gone. He also knew that if John and Faith both were gone, he would claim ownership anyway. He also knew that he wanted Faith. He needed her. She is all about which he could think. He dreamt of her. He was a man obsessed. He needed to have a talk with Faith. Louis left the office with one thing on his mind. He must see Faith tonight.

Louis arrived at the plantation after dark in the morning hours. Everyone was asleep. He let himself in, went up the stairs, and knew he must see Faith. He would not even wake her. He just wanted to be near her. He eased her door open. The moonlight was pouring into her room through her window. He could see her asleep on her back in a white, cotton nightgown. Her breasts rose with each breath she took. He mesmerized aback at how beautiful she looked. The animal inside him was barely containing itself. He was a beast waiting to pounce and ravage her. In his mind, he could see himself mounting her and grunting against her and he knew if she fought him, he would love it. He wanted her to fight him, so he could treat her like the whore that she was. As he went to walk near the bed, a sound caught his attention. He backed out of the room, eased back down the stairs just in time to see Maw Sally scurrying past. She did not see him. He let himself out of the house. He knew it was not the right time, but just the sight of her pushed his animal instincts to the back, for the time being.

Maw Sally felt like she needed to go check on Faith. She had learned in her years on this earth to trust your instincts. She had the feeling that something evil was a lurking. She checked in on Faith and she was okay. She sat in the rocking chair watching over her for a few hours. As she headed back to her bed, she saw the Ebony statue in the foyer. The statue just made her think of her Ebony. She had named her daughter Ebony because she had wanted her to be strong. She wanted her to be a polished woman, yet strong, like the dense black wood of ebony. Ebony had given the statue to Ms. Victoria as a thank you for helping them when she came to Edwards Plantation that frigid winter. Ms. Victoria tried not to accept the gift, however, Ebony insisted. It has stood there all these years. Polished, proud and beautiful and was always Maw Sally's reminder of her beautiful daughter and grandson.

Chapter 12

The Plan

As Vayne rode away from the plantation and headed back to the ship, his mind was troubled. He knew that he had to figure out how to fix this situation. There were many loose ends that he needed to figure out. He would get with Trent, and they would have to come up with a plan to get the paperwork. He did not know what this animal was up to, but he knew it was no good. He also knew that there were things that he needed to tell Faith about himself and his past and he hoped that she would understand.

The next morning Vayne headed to Trent's cabin. As he approached the cabin, he saw Trent mounting his horse. Trent looked up as he heard him approaching.

"I figured you would be back here this morning, after all that we found out yesterday."

Vayne grunted, "Yes we have got to figure this one out friend and quick."

Trent nodded, "I was headed into town. Do you want to join me? I was going to see if I could find this Louis character. It looks like me and you both have issues with him."

"Yes. We need to keep our distance right now, but we need to get an idea of this guy and what he is doing and what he is up to," Vayne said.

As they rode into town, both men felt the pressure to fix this. Trent wanted revenge for Daisy and Vayne wanted to keep Faith safe and help her family. Both men knew that they usually had a common interest, and this time was no different. When they approached town, they decided to stay together and walk through town and not draw attention to themselves. They were across the street from Edwards Banking when Vayne spotted John Edwards entering. Vayne knew that he was starting his workday, and he would keep an eye on him as well. As they were watching Vayne nudged Trent with his elbow.

"That fellow right there. The one walking with the hat and brown coat on."

Trent looked over as he leaned against the railing, "Yeah, what about him?"

"That is the fellow that hurt your Daisy. That is Faith's cousin, Louis."

Trent went to walk across the road and Vayne touched his arm, "No. We cannot do that yet. We need to get everything settled and the paperwork and then you can have him. Not yet, buddy. However, you will get him."

Trent understood and eased back, "Yeah. Now is not the time."

Louis entered the bank and walked into John's office just as he was sitting down.

"Have you given any thought as to what I asked you about Faith?" Louis asked.

John looked up, "Yes, I have. It is not going to happen. Why don't you stop all this nonsense? Why are you doing this? We have always been good to you. Your poor mother would be so disappointed in you."

Louis sat down across from John's desk, "My poor mother was weak. She appeased you. She never got what she deserved. You may have taken care of her but she never got what she deserved."

"What exactly did your mother warrant Louis? She was taken care of. When she died of the fever, she had the best of everything."

"She was weak. She did not realize that she could have gotten more," Louis said.

"Louis, what do you want? What can I do to placate you?"

"I want it all. The bank, the plantation, and Faith."

John wanted to reach over the desk and kill him in this very moment, "Faith is off limits. You are sick Louis."

Louis laughed, "You're sick if you think I will give up."

John looked at Louis with a dead stare, "If you think, for one minute, that I will allow you to wed my daughter, your cousin, you are sadly mistaken. It will not happen. It will be over my dead body."

"That can be arranged, dear uncle."

"Do what you got to do Louis. Just be ready for a fight when you do. Now if you will excuse me, I have work to do."

Louis got up and walked from the bank. He walked to the end of the street and crossed over to the Saloon. As he walked to the Saloon, Vayne and Trent crossed over and followed him inside. They kept a safe, quiet distance from him. He walked over to the bar and ordered a whiskey.

"Where is Daisy?" he asked the bartender.

"She ain't here no more."

Hearing him ask about Daisy made Trent's blood boil. He kept his cool at the far corner.

"You got any redheaded whores?"

Vayne felt his body stiffen. He wanted to rip his throat out. He kept his cool and Trent nudged him to get his attention and shook his head. Vayne flexed his jaw. Trent could tell by the look that if Vayne had half the chance, this man would be dead.

Bartender shrugged.

Louis got up and left the bar. Vayne and Trent downed their whiskeys and followed him out. As Louis left the bar, he spit and headed around to the back of the building. They kept a safe distance behind him. As he walked the alley, he entered the back door. They followed him, peered into the window to the left of the door, and saw Louis slide a canning shelf to the left and go inside the wall. They both were puzzled as to what he was doing.

"We need to see what is in there," Vayne said.

Trent nodded in agreement, "We need to come back later, when we know he is gone."

The men eased back to their horses and rode out of town. They headed to the ship. They needed to sit down, get a plan, and get to work on this. They had dealt with a lot over the years together and knew what they needed to do to get started. The first thing was to get a strategy.

They boarded the ship and went down to Vayne's quarters. Vayne fixed them both a drink.

"We need to go back and see what that was all about. A secret room is a telltale sign of where things are kept you would want no one to get their hands on," Trent said.

"Yes. We will do that tonight. We need to start watching the plantation at night as well. This Louis is capable of anything, and we need to be ready. Daisy is safe. He obviously does not know where she is. We need to make sure Faith is safe," Vayne said.

"I agree. We can take turns watching the Plantation. We need to have one of us on Louis as well."

"I will take the plantation tonight and you can see what that room is all about. Just be careful," Vayne Said.

It was dark outside by the time they finished discussing strategy. Trent headed toward town and Vayne went toward The Plantation.

As Vayne neared the plantation, he felt anxious. He was not sure why, but he felt the hairs on the back of his neck stand up. He stopped and looked around. He did not see anyone. He was sure there was something lurking but just did not know what. He found a good spot up on the hill near a grove of trees and decided it was good. He got off his horse and took a seat leaning back against a tree.

As Trent neared town, he slowed down. He tethered his horse just outside of town and walked the rest of the way on foot. He went down the alleyway, took a left and stalled for a moment to make sure he did not hear any noise. He had brought a lantern with him. He went to the doorway and listened again for any sounds coming from within. He gently as possible slid the canning shelf to the side and went inside. He stopped and lit his lantern. He was shocked at what he saw. It was a makeshift office. Desk, shelves, a chair, evens a whiskey bar. He walked over to the desk and opened the drawers. He shuffled through the papers. He could not believe what he saw. He found several papers where Louis had been practicing signing John Edwards's name. He held his breath hoping that he would find the other papers with the seal on them. He opened the second drawer and found nothing. He opened the third drawer and found a scroll. He opened the scroll and there they were. It was the paperwork showing Louis as owner of Edwards Banking and Edwards Plantation. Trent felt his heart race. He shoved the scroll into his jacket, blew out his lantern, and made his way out of the office. As he was fixing to exit, he heard a sound outside. He slid back against the wall in the dark and listened. He could hear talking. It was a male and female. He heard a thud. He could hear Louis talking.

"You like that? You like being treated like the dirty little whore you are?" Louis gritted out of his teeth.

"Please stop," Trent heard a female voice say lightly.

"No I won't stop. Beg me to hurt you?" Louis said.

Trent could barely contain himself. He knew he needed to keep a low profile, but this lowlife was hurting another woman. Trent braced himself and his mind raced at what he should do. Trent knew that he had to do the right thing. Trent eased around the door so that he could see Louis's shadow on top of the woman. He lunged and knocked him to the floor. He kicked him in the stomach, snatched the girl up, pushed her out the door, and yelled, "Run!" Trent started to run and Louis grabbed his foot. Trent tripped, caught his balance, kicked Louis in the jaw, and threw himself out of the door. He knew that Louis did not see his face or know who he was. Right now, that is.

Trent made it back to his cabin in record time. He scared Daisy as he burst through the door.

"Trent, you scared the dickens out of me! What is going on?"

"I found the paperwork that Vayne and Faith need!" he laughed.

Daisy's eyes got big, "You didn't kill him, did you?"

"Not yet. He does not know who I am or that I have them. He got a good kick to the jaw and stomach though," Trent was laughing.

"Lord Trent. You are going to be the death of me!"

"I lucked up tonight. I knew with me and Vayne working together, something would happen sooner rather than later. It always does!"

As Vayne sat quietly, he started to smell smoke, the distinct odor of cigar smoke. He could tell it was coming from behind him. His back was up against the tree and he was not sure from which direction the smell was coming. The right or the left. Vayne decided to call whomever it was to show themselves.

"Why don't you come on out? I smell your cigar."

Al stepped from around the tree and into Vayne's line of sight. "Hello there."

"What brings you out this time of night?" Vayne asked,

As Al looked at Vayne, he knew exactly who he was. He had the same eyes, the same hair, and the exact same features. "I have heard of you. You are Vayne Lafitte."

"That is right. I do not know who you are though."

"You would not know me. They kept you hid from me. I knew your mother though," Al said taking a drag of his cigar.

Vayne felt the color drain from his face, "My mother?"

"Yes. Your mother was the half breed named Ebony, right?"

Vayne felt the rage immediately when it came up, "I would advise you not to speak of my mother that way," he said low and calm.

Al chuckled, "I see you have the same spunk that she did when I impregnated her with my seed."

Vayne felt the blood come to his face in a rage of fury, "When you what?" Vayne said calmly.

Al chuckled again as he walked toward Vayne, "Yes you have not figured it out yet? It is nice to meet you son."

As Al said this, Vayne lunged forward and forced his saber into the belly of Al. The force sent Al falling backward, but Vayne caught him by the neck, jerking him forward into his face, and pulled the saber up. Al started to gurgle his words. Vayne leaned down into the short, fat man's face, "You are no father of mine. My mother was both to me. Anyone who dares to disrespect her will be run through."

Vayne pulled his knife and let Al fall to the ground. As he cleaned his knife, he said to Al calmly, "I will tie you to this tree and leave you here for the vultures. Your death will be long and tortuous. Just because you forced yourself upon my mother and impregnated her does not make you a tough man or a father. You never had a son, and you never will have one now," as he said this, he picked Al up, moved him further into the woods, so as to not be seen, tied him to the tree and left him there to die.

Vayne leveled his breathing. His mind was racing, but he knew that he had a job to do, and he must keep an eye on Faith. He needed to keep her safe. *His poor mother. What she must have endured at the hands of this man.* Vayne felt tears rise up but pushed them back. He was not one to show his emotions, even when alone. It had been a long time since Vayne had killed anyone. This kill did not bother him. It was the thoughts of his mother that bothered him. Knowing what this animal had done to her, how he was conceived, knowing that his mother loved him despite it. He did not remember a lot of his mother, but he did know that she loved him. He felt it and the feeling is forever with him. It made sense now why he never knew who his father was. Why there was never a father figure around. Vayne did not remember what happened to his mother. He had no recollection of anything after leaving the Plantation on that day. He was a baby of two or three years. He also has no memory of how Ms. Alma ended up with him. It is time to have a conversation with Ms. Alma. When he left home, it did not seem that important at the time. However, as he has gotten older, this is information that he longs for.

Chapter 13
Truth Seeking

The next morning Vayne rode to Trent's cabin to discuss the plans. Trent met him at the door, "Man, Vayne. You do not look so good."

"It has been a long night. Did you find anything?"

Trent smiled, "I found the forged paperwork."

Vayne sat up in his chair. "You don't say?"

"I sure did. I also had a run in with Louis, but he is still alive and never saw my face. That man is seriously evil. I interrupted him attacking another female. Let us just say I intervened, got her out of there and I got out of there," Trent said, shaking his head.

"He did not see your face or know who you were?"

Trent shook his head, "Nope. He never knew what hit him. He is feeling it this morning though," Trent chuckled.

"Well, I had a run in with one of his men last night," Vayne said.

"What happened?" Trent asked.

"He is dead. He did not fare as well as ole Louis did," Vayne said. He did not go into what happened and who Al was. That was not a conversation for now. That was something personal that he did not care to share at this time.

"What should our next step be?" Trent asked, offering Vayne a mug of coffee.

"I need to go and speak with Faith and her father. That will need to be their decision."

Trent shook his head in agreement, "Just let me know what you want to do," he handed Vayne the scroll.

Vayne left the cabin and headed to see Faith. He needed to speak with her. He needed to give them the paperwork and be honest and let her decide if she wants to be with him knowing he is a pirate and what he does to help others in need. He knew that it was not fair to let her be with him and her not truly know what she was getting herself into.

When he arrived at the plantation, Faith met him on the porch, "Is your father home?"

Faith looked at him concerned, "He is. I will get him for you."

Vayne nodded at her, "I need to speak to you both together and you by yourself later."

Faith Nodded, "Father, Vayne is here. He needs to speak with us."

John invited him in, and they went to the study. He turned to Vayne, "What can I help you with?"

He took the scroll from his pocket and handed it to him. "I have something I think you would want."

John unrolled the scroll, stumbled back, and sat down.

"Father what's wrong?" Faith asked concerned.

"Nothing is wrong my sweet girl. Vayne just handed me the forged paperwork that Louis had for the Plantation and the bank," John smiled with relief.

Faith looked at Vayne with her mouth gaping open, "How in the world did you get those?"

Vayne told her and Mr. Edwards about the plans. He told them what Trent did to get the paperwork. He left out the part about Al. He wanted to discuss that with Faith alone and in private.

"Mr. Edwards, if you don't mind, I would like to spend some time with Faith today."

"Of course not, you spend all the time you need. I cannot thank you enough for this. I will meet with Louis shortly."

"Mr. Edwards, I would be careful if I were you. I would not meet with him. I would let him come to you. He is a sick man."

John just nodded.

Vayne reached down and got Faith's hand. John smiled to himself. The two walked outside and down the steps. He wanted to walk and talk at the same time. He did not want to ride and be on separate horses. After last night, he just wanted to be near her. He wanted to feel her hand in his. He needed her. She did not know how much he truly needed her right now. They turned and went down toward the creek. They walked for a long while and said nothing. Faith could sense that Vayne had a heavy heart.

"Faith, I need to talk to you about me. I need to make sure you know what you are getting yourself into with me."

Faith stopped and moved in front of him and took both of his hands.

"I killed a man last night," he looked at her waiting for her expression to change. It did not. She just kept looking at him intently.

"What happened?" she asked.

"I need to start from the beginning. Trent and I decided that someone needed to watch over you and your father at night. I was watching from the hilltop when this man walked up. I recognized him from town. Faith, this man said vile things about my mother and told me he was my father. I killed him. He was not my father. Mother was both. I cannot explain my thoughts, but he got what was coming to him and I don't feel bad about it."

Faith felt guilty. She knew more about Vayne's family than he did at this point. It made her heart ache. She put her head down.

"I know this may push you away from me and I understand. You also need to know that I have a ship. Not a boat, as I lead you to believe. I have been expelled from Texas and I came here. I take from the wicked, who steal, and I give the cargo I get to the less fortunate who cannot fend for themselves or are having a hard time," he looked at her intently as she spoke these words to her.

"Faith looked up at him. I admire you, Vayne. There is nothing you could say to me that will change that. I feel your loyalty. I know you are a man of substance. I know that you are a man of honor. That man you killed; he deserved it. There are some things that I need to tell you also."

She drew him over to sit down on a log so that she could face him. She was not sure how he was going to react to what she was about to tell him.

"I have information that I found out about your mother and your grandmother. I was going to tell you, but I needed to make sure it was the right time. Your mother and grandmother came to our plantation when you were just a small child. I know you remember this because you told me about it. Well, your grandmother was sick at the time and was too ill to travel when your mother left with you. I do not know what happened to your mother, but I can tell you that your grandmother is still alive," she was looking at him intently in his eyes.

"My grandmother is alive. How do you know this?"

"I know because I know her. I have known her my entire life, but I did not know she was your grandmother until a few days ago."

"What do you know about my father?" he asked.

"All I know about him is that your grandmother and your mother were in a village. Men came through the village and were burning everything. They were murdering the men and raping the women. That is when your mother was attacked," she said quietly.

Vayne felt sick. The visions running through his head just made him sick, "Does my grandmother know I am here? Are you sure she is my grandmother?"

Faith got him by the hand and led him back toward home, "She does not know you are here and yes, I am sure that she is your grandmother. Come with me. It is time you two came back together."

Faith and Vayne walked hand in hand back to the house. Faith walked in the backdoor and called out to Maw Sally. May Sally came to the door and pushed open the screen.

"Maw Sally, I have someone I want you to meet."

Maw Sally looked down the steps at Vayne. She took a couple of steps back. She would know those eyes, lips, and hair anywhere. "You look just like your mother," she said choking back sobs.

Vayne bounded up the steps and wrapped his arms around her, "Grandmother. If I had known you were this close, this whole time I would have never stayed away."

"Child, I thought you were dead. Where is your mother?"

"I don't know. I remember nothing from the day we left here," Vayne said.

Faith looked at the two reuniting and the lump in her throat got bigger as she saw tears sliding down Vayne's cheeks. He did not attempt to hide them. He hugged his grandmother until Maw Sally told him to come inside, sit, and talk with her. Faith followed them inside. She felt happy that the only mother she knew and the man that she may love found his family again.

"Chile where have you been? Where did you come from? Where did you grow up?" Maw Sally asked.

"I was raised by a lady named Ms. Alma. I do not have any recollection of when I got there, I just remember being with her. I left her home before I was sixteen to go out into the world and find my way. I always felt like something was missing, but now I realize I was searching for you and my mother."

Faith was astonished, "Ms. Alma raised you?"

Vayne nodded his head.

"Ms. Alma may have answers about your mother," Faith said.

"She may. I need to talk to her. I need to find out what she knows," Vayne said.

Vayne hugged Maw Sally again, "Grandmother I have missed you so much."

"Chile I will never let you out of my sight again. I am glad you found me," Maw Sally said.

John Edwards walked into the house and saw Maw Sally sitting with Vayne with his hands in hers. "Mr. Edwards, I want you to meet my grandson."

John cleared his throat, "I have met him. I see Faith got you acquainted. I knew it would happen when the timing was right. Vayne you are welcome at Edwards Plantation at any time. I am forever in your debt."

Vayne just nodded. Overcome with emotion, he did not have the words to speak, "Grandmother, I need to go and see what I can find out from Ms. Alma. I need to see what, if anything, she knows about Mother. I will be back as soon as I finish speaking to her."

"Vayne, please come back to me," Maw Sally said.

"I will. Soon."

Faith walked him out to the porch to see him off. He bent down and kissed her slowly and hard on the lips. In that moment, Faith knew she was his and Vayne knew he was hers.

Vayne arrived at the bookstore before it closed. He walked in, the bell rang, and Ms. Alma came from the back. "Vayne! How are you?"

He looked at her, "Please sit. We need to talk."

Ms. Alma looked at him. She knew it was serious by his tone, "What's wrong?"

"I killed my father last night."

The color drained from her face, "You what?"

"He was saying vile things about my mother and what he did to her and said he was my father and I killed him. Do you know anything about my parents? I was only sixteen when I left your home and those things did not seem important back then, but I am asking now."

"That was a long time ago. I do not think…" He cut her off.

"It matters to me," he said.

"What happened to my mother? How did I come to live with you?"

Ms. Alma could barely speak. She was having a tough time finding her words, "My son brought you to me."

"Who was your son?" Vayne asked.

"The man you killed, sadly, was my son. The disappointment, which he was. Vayne, he was not a good man, and I am sad to say that. He was too much like his father. I tried to protect you. I did protect you. When I found out what he had done to poor Ebony, I took you and he never saw you again. You were my grandson, and I wanted to keep you safe and love you. I did not want you to know how you came to be here. I did not want you to know the ugliness that my son, the person I created, had caused. He was a sick man. So I kept you hid and tucked away until you decided to leave," she said wiping her eyes.

Vayne ran his fingers through his hair. "Where is my mother?"

"I don't know dear. Al said that she was killed. I do not know if that was true or not. I just know that he showed up here one day with you and I overheard him bragging to his friends about what had happened in that village and that he got a son out of it. I took you and left."

Vayne wanted to be angry with her, but he could not. He knew that she loved him and that she did what she thought was right. She protected him. She had given him a good life. He kissed her on the cheek and bid her goodbye. He could hear her crying as he walked out of the door and shut it behind him. Vayne knew there was only one place he wanted to be right now. That place was at Edwards Plantation with his grandmother and the woman that he loved.

Chapter 14
Laying Low

Louis Edwards was pacing his make shift office. The paperwork was gone. He knew that whomever it was that interrupted his good time was the one that took it. He knew that it was not his uncle because he would not have the guts to do that. It was not Al, because he would know that fat tub of lard anywhere. He had not seen Al for quite some time. He was probably drunk somewhere sleeping it off. He should pay Dexter a visit at the bank. He is the only person he could think of that would have anything to gain, besides his uncle.

Dexter was leaving the bank when he saw Louis cross the street toward him, "Mr. Edwards, what I can help you with? The bank is closed."

Louis grabbed him by the arm and led him around back, "Where is the paperwork, Dexter?"

"What paperwork?" Dexter asked confused.

"I know that was you the other night that attacked me and took the paperwork from my office," Louis growled.

"I did no such thing and what office are you talking about? You do not have an office at the bank?"

Louis pushed Dexter into the canning room, slid over the shelf, opened his office door, and pushed Dexter inside. Louis was not going to let Dexter walk away from this. He pulled out his knife, lunged it into Dexter's throat, and ripped it from left to right. The red sticky blood flowed from his neck. It did not phase Louis. Dexter fell to the floor holding his neck, wide eyed while gurgling. Louis looked down at him and said, "That will show you not to cross me. I am done messing around."

Dexter thought before his last breath, *he is truly a mad man.*

Louis finished burying Dexter. He was angry because Al usually handled this for him. He must do it all these days. *Some help they are! Dexter was gone now, so he only had to deal with Al. Al could help him until he no longer served the purpose,* he thought.

Louis had a plan. He wanted to destroy John Edwards, and he wanted to destroy Faith Edwards. Slow, hard, and brutal and that is what he was setting his mind to do. He would take them down. First John Edwards fast and quick but he was going to enjoy torturing Faith and he would do it long and slow. He would go after them when they least expected it. They would never see it coming. He would lay low on this idea for a while and then would pounce. Louis planned to leave town for a while and lay low. He would leave now.

Chapter 15
Preparations

The days turned into weeks. Faith and Vayne had seen each other daily as well as Vayne and Maw Sally. They had not seen Louis in weeks, and it was a relief to Faith and John. They knew that he had run and that was fine by them. Faith loved feeling calm again, and she knew, without a doubt, she was truly in love with Vayne Lafitte. He had been here almost daily over the last month, and she savored every moment.

Faith was at Daisy's helping her with the last of the details for the wedding. Faith had grown close to both Trent and Daisy. "We almost have everything in order for your beautiful day," Faith said while helping Daisy build the arch.

"I know and I am so excited. I cannot tell you how much I appreciate your help and friendship," Daisy said.

"I have enjoyed it. This is the first wedding I have ever been a part of. It is exciting. I am so happy for you and Trent."

"Since we are talking about weddings, what about you and Vayne?" Daisy asked, looking at Faith and raising an eyebrow.

Faith turned red, smiled at the same time, and looked up. "You would have to ask Mr. Lafitte about that."

Daisy was stunned that Faith all but said she would marry him. "So, you would marry him if he asked you?"

"In a heartbeat and without a second thought," Faith grinned.

Daisy felt her heart swell with happiness. "I am so glad to hear it. To hear Trent tell it, he feels the same way about you."

Faith sighed, "To be honest, I can feel he loves me. I just do not know if he is ready to be a husband just yet."

"He might just surprise you," Daisy said.

The two women stood up to attach the arch made from wisteria onto the post. It looked beautiful. The wedding would be at the cabin beside the stream. It was a beautiful site. The wildflowers were plentiful, the water was clear, and the wisteria was fresh and purple. The stream was a beautiful backdrop with the sound of water lightly trickling. It was a perfect site for a wedding.

"Well tomorrow is the big day. I have something to give you," she reached out and handed Daisy a pendant with a baby blue stone. Faith did not even know what stone it was, but she knew that it used to be her mothers. Faith never had a sibling, she knew that Daisy was the closest thing she would ever have to a sister, and she wanted her to have it.

Daisy gasped, "I cannot accept this. It is just too much."

Faith hugged her, "Don't be silly. I want you to have it. It was my mothers, and you are the only sister I will ever have. Please take it. It is my gift to you."

Daisy felt tears come down her cheeks. She hugged Faith and did not want to let go. "Thank you. I will treasure it always."

"It is your something blue," Faith said.

As the girls were wrapping up their heart-felt hugs, Vayne and Trent walked down to the spring.

"It looks good ladies," Trent said.

"Why thank you sir," Faith answered.

Vayne walked up behind Faith, wrapped his arms around her, and rested his chin in her head. Faith could feel his warmth on her back and feel his heartbeat. She had never felt as safe as she did with this man. She turned toward him and gave him a squeeze.

"Should we be heading out?" Vayne asked.

Faith smiled, "Yes I think we should."

Trent looked over and tilted his head, "Why you running off? It is not dark yet."

"We need to get back early. We will be back tomorrow for your big day," he slapped Trent on the back.

Faith and Vayne headed out. They shared a horse when they came to the cabin this time. Faith secretly was glad. She liked being near him. On the way, back to the plantation, Vayne asked, "You want to go see my ship?"

"Are you sure you are ready for that?" Faith said jokingly.

"I think I can manage it," he said as he bent down and nibbled on her ear.

Faith sucked in a breath and moved closer to him. They set out for the ship. When Faith saw it in the distance, she could not believe the beauty. She had never seen anything like it. It took her by surprise. *He was right,* she thought, *it was not a boat.* As they got closer, she started the notice the intricate detail of the ship. She immediately noticed the name, "The Lady Ebony."

"Let me help you down and I will show you around," Vayne said.

As they climbed up on the ship, Faith could not help but wonder what wonders this ship had saw. Where had it been? What had it seen?

"She is a beauty!" Faith said.

Vayne smiled but said nothing. Faith looked around and she noticed the crewmembers and was a little shocked. She knew that he would never let anything happen to her, but these men looked gruff and tough. As if reading her mind, Vayne said, "Do not worry. They are friendly. They would not hurt you."

"Good to know," she said.

"Paddy, is all on task for the delivery next week?"

"Aye Sir," he said in true Paddy fashion.

"Good. You men can take off. We are going down to my quarters for a bit," Vayne said.

Faith and Vayne headed down to his quarters. Faith noticed how clean and pristine it was. There was a small writing desk on one wall made of mahogany and she saw it had been recently. There was a four-poster bed on the other wall was shelves filled with books. Faith could tell that he was full of surprises, and she had only scratched the surface with this beautiful man. As she was turning to look, she felt him staring at her. He went and sat down on the bed.

"Come here," he said.

Faith walked over to him. The look in his eyes made her blood stir. She had not seen this look before. As she walked over to him, he stood up and circled behind her. He bent down just enough to reach her neck, and she felt his tongue move along the inside of her neck lightly. Faith thought she would burst. She took in a breath, and she could feel herself tremble. Vayne reached down, wrapped his arms around her waist, and tugged her closer to him. His could smell the sweetness in her hair and taste the saltiness on her skin from the sweat from the ride over. Vayne knew that he loved this woman. He had been with many women in his day, but none did this to him. He must stop. He did not want to take her until they were wed. It was the only thing he could give to her, besides his love, that he had never given to another woman. He respected her and wanted to save her until that night. However, he also wanted her to feel what she had to look forward too.

Faith turned toward him. It was her time to take charge. She knew what she wanted, and she knew that could get him to do anything she wanted. She took his hands and placed them on the side of her face. Vayne sucked in when she did this. He felt like he was going to explode. He felt the familiar ache and groaned. Faith pulled him down toward her so that she could reach his mouth. She kissed him softly. Vayne felt like she had him under a spell.

"Faith, we have got to stop," he said.

"I don't want to stop. Not yet," she said breathing hard against his lips.

"We have to. I do not want to take you this way. Not like this," he said with his lips just inches from hers.

"Don't you want me?" she asked.

Vayne groaned and laughed at the same time, "Of course I do. You have no clue how much I do want you. I will have you, but I want you to know what you have to look forward to," he said.

"Look forward too?" she asked.

"Faith, when it is finally our time and I make you my wife, I want to make you feel passion like you have never known possible. You have no clue the ecstasy that awaits you. I will know every inch of you from head to toe and I will know exactly what you like. I want you to know that this is nothing to be afraid of."

Faith felt her heart start to race. She was excited and a little scared at the same time. She had never been with a man sexually before and she knew that Vayne would be her first. She knew that he could either make her the happiest woman on earth or shatter her with one blow. She did not know how to respond to him. She did not know what to say. She backed away slowly. Her head was spinning, and her heart was racing. She had never had her body react this way before.

"Well, Mr. Lafitte, maybe we better get me home," she said shyly.

"I think that may be a good idea," he said.

As they started to walk out of his quarters, he reached down and put his arms around her facing him. He bent down and picked her up with ease. "Kiss me Faith," he said.

Faith leaned in and touched his lips with hers and they both felt an electricity like the one they had never experienced before. Vayne grunted, sat her down, got her hand and they headed toward the deck. "Yes, we need to get you home and fast," Vayne said with a laugh.

Chapter 16
The Wedding

It was a beautiful fall day. There was a gentle breeze blowing. As promised, Vayne and Faith arrived at the cabin early to help get ready for the wedding.

Faith dressed in a white satin dress with pink flowers embroidered in the hem that fell just below the knee. The dress showed just a hint of cleavage and the dress fit her frame perfectly. Her red hair was loosely pinned on top of her head with curls dangling around her face with baby's breath scattered throughout.

Vayne was handsome in his black attire. Tight pants that stretched across the hips and tied at the waist, that Faith could not keep her eyes off him. He wore a white shirt with the sleeves tapered at the wrists. He wore no tie and left the first two buttons undone. The shirt stretched across his muscular chest and broad shoulders to perfection. He did not wear a hat and his dark hair curled around the nape of his neck and ears slightly.

Trent wore the usual, black suit and black tie, with a Black bowler hat, tilted, just so slightly.

The black pants tapered at the waist, were perfectly matched with his black boots. He wore a white shirt under his suit with the cuff links Vayne had given him as a wedding gift.

Daisy wore a simple, white, lace gown that dipped in the front to show her full breasts. The dress had an empire waist and flowed down past her feet with a subtle train. It was simplicity and elegance at its best. Her long blonde hair was back in a French twist with baby's breath, and she had fastened the light blue pendant into her hair. Her bouquet was wildflowers and baby's breath with a sprig of wisteria. She had on flat, white, satin slippers.

In attendance at the wedding were John Edwards, Maw Sally, and Ms. Alma. This was the only family that Trent and Daisy had. John Edwards would officiate the wedding.

The ceremony was beautiful and typical. After the ceremony, the wedding party headed to Edwards Plantation to continue the festivities with roasted pig, potatoes, carrots, and a three-tier wedding cake donated from Maw Sally herself. Vayne made a toast to the couple.

As the celebration was winding down, it was time for the bride and groom the throw the bouquet and leave. Of course, the only eligible woman there, besides Maw Sally and Ms. Alma was Faith. She caught the bouquet, and everyone made a fuss.

John surprised Trent and Daisy with a covered carriage decorated ornately as their wedding night gift. It was adorned with wisteria and grape vines.

Vayne and Faith had secretly decorated their cabin and left a feast and drinks for them as a surprise when they returned home. Everyone clapped as they drove away to start their journey as husband and wife.

As Vayne and Faith watched them drive away in the carriage, Vayne reached down and took her hand. "Come with me," he said.

They walked back toward the house and Ms. Alma, Maw Sally, and John Edwards were standing around talking. As they approached everyone turned with a smile, as Faith looked up, Vayne knelt in front of her on one knee and took out a box, "Faith Edwards will you marry me?"

Faith looked over at her father and then at Maw Sally. They both smiled and nodded their heads in agreement. As tears flowed down her face, "Yes, I will marry you. I love you."

Vayne took the ring from the box. He bought an emerald ring just for her because it matched her eyes. He slid the ring on her finger, as he did so, he swore to himself that he would protect her with his life, and she would never be without love.

Faith gasped, "Oh no. What about Trent and Daisy? They are going to be so upset they did not get to be here for this."

Vayne smiled, "They already knew about it. We have their blessing. I talked to your father and got his permission before I asked you. I have wanted to do this for a while, I could not find the right time, and I figured it would be a perfect time with your father, Maw Sally, and Ms. Alma here all together. What better time than now?"

"You were absolutely right," she said as she walked up and kissed him.

John Edwards cleared his throat and walked over to them both with tears in his eyes, "Welcome to the family son. When is the big day?" he asked.

Vayne glanced at Faith, "You will have to ask your daughter," he said through laughter.

"As soon as possible," she said smiling and wrapping her arms around both men.

"I must go out of town to make a delivery next week. We can start planning and getting everything ready. I agree with Faith. The sooner. The better. We can plan it after I get back. I should be gone three, five days at the latest," Vayne said.

Maw Sally walked over and hugged both Faith and Vayne, "I have my grandson back and the little girl I watched grow up into a beautiful woman. My cup runneth over," She said with tears in her eyes, "This ole woman is happy."

Ms. Alma walked up slowly and placed her hand on Vayne's shoulder, "I love you, my grandson. I hope you can forgive this ole woman for not telling you all you needed to know years ago," she said.

Vayne hugged her, "You were protecting me. I know that. It was forgiven the moment you told me."

They each bid goodnight. Vayne walked Faith to the corner of the house into the shadows. He wanted to be alone with her. For just a little while.

"I love you, Faith. I will be back soon and when I do, we can start our life together."

She smiled and snuggled under his arm, "I cannot wait. I am so happy."

"Me too. It was so hard not to tell you last night, but I knew if I did, it would ruin what I had planned for tonight. Your father would not have been happy with me if I had sprung it on you then."

"Last night was nice," Faith said.

Vayne grunted and rubbed his nose in her hair, "Yes it was. I cannot wait to make you mine completely in every way."

Faith felt herself grow hot. She could not wait either. She hoped she could please him. She did not know if she would understand what to do. As if reading her mind, he said, "Do not be nervous. I will teach you. Before you know it, you may be teaching me some things," he groaned against her ear. "Faith, you have no clue what you do to me. You make me feel weak but make me want to rip your clothes off at the same time."

Faith leaned harder into him. "I have never had these feelings that you stir in me. I am not sure what to do with them," she said.

"You will figure it out. Trust me. After we are wed, I will show you just what to do with them," he said as he pushed his lips onto hers.

Faith licked his tongue with hers and ran her fingers through the hair at the nape of his neck. She traced her fingers down his back to his hips. She touched his arms and hands. She had her eyes closed and Vayne stopped to watch her. She felt the muscles in his arms and the veins in his hands bulge. Vayne knew that she was memorizing him with her hands as he had her with his eyes. She traced his jawline and touched his lips. Vayne sucked in his breath.

"You have no clue what you do to me. You are innocent in a way that is so damn seductive," he groaned.

Faith stepped back. She felt dizzy. She wanted to be with him so bad, but she knew that she had to wait. It was not time yet. She knew that the longer they waited the better it would be. She knew that once he was her husband, it was no holds barred and he would teach her things that she never knew was possible.

Vayne walked Faith to the door and kissed her gently good night, "I will see you soon."

Faith shut the door, leaned against it, and had to make herself walk up the stairs to her room. She was giddy. She was engaged and genuinely happy.

Chapter 17
The Voyage

Vayne knew that he needed to get the cargo delivered and get back as fast as he could. He had never been in such a hurry before. He liked being on his ship and out in the ocean. He just knew now that he wanted Faith to be with him. He did not like leaving her. Louis had not been seen for weeks now. He still did not feel good about it. He had families depending on him for the goods he was going to deliver. He would just port, unload, and get back home.

Vayne dressed in his usual "pirate" attire. He donned his tricorn on his head with his white poet blouse and black breeches. He went up onto deck and helped the men to ready the ship. The black and white skull and crossbones flag was hoisted. This usually deterred other vessels to come near the Lady Ebony. He liked it that way.

The cannons were placed strategically around the ship. They were rarely fired but used to deter visitors. The crew used langrage spikes placed around the ship, in case they were needed, instead of the cannon balls. There were barrels on the deck of the ship. This is where supplies were stored. They had even smuggled children in these barrels when they needed to get them to safety. There was also a sounding lead on board to determine water depth, when necessary, especially when he needed to make swift change and hide if need be.

The ship set sail for the Isla de Cedros. It would not take but two days to get there if they did not hit harsh weather. A village there was extremely poor and needed the cargo in order to survive. A hurricane took out most everything on the island as well as their small fishing boats, which they used to fish and keep plentiful food supply. Vayne took cargo to these people every year around the same time for the past few years. The people were very friendly and respected the members of his crew.

After a review of the supplies and making sure the ship was ready, Vayne instructed Paddy and other crewmembers to raise the sails. The sails were hoisted. This was usually Vayne's favorite part, but he just had a nagging feeling. He did not want to go. He shoved the thought in the back of his mind and set about his work. The crew was, and they angled the sails just right to get out of the harbor. It was only a few, and they were out into open waters.

The skies were, and they were on their way. Vayne loved the feel of the salt-water air on his skin.

"Paddy, at this rate, we will be a one-day voyage at the most," Vayne said.

"Aye. Maybe so. I got the feeling in me bones we might be in for some dangerous weather sooner or later."

"Looks like clear skies to me," Vayne said looking around, but he had learned a long time ago to trust Paddy's bones."

Back at the Plantation, Faith was still giddy and planning a wedding in her head. She knew exactly what she wanted. She had not told Vayne yet, but she knew he would love it. She could not wait to show Daisy her ring. She would wear her mother's wedding dress. She always knew she would wear this dress. It was in the trunk in her room. She had even tried it on. It fit like a glove. She even had her mother's white satin gloves that covered her arm to the elbow. She was so ready to become Mrs. Lafitte. She had never been surer of anything in her life.

Maw Sally bustled into her room, "Chile what are you smiling at? You grinning to yourself like you got thoughts running through your mind," she said.

"I am thinking about my mother's wedding dress and how I cannot wait to marry your grandson."

"Well, I cannot blame you there child. They are good thoughts."

Faith smiled as she got up from her perch, "Well I am going to run into town and see Ms. Alma. I wanted to help her around the bookstore. I am trying to keep myself busy while Vayne is gone. It will help the time pass by faster."

"Child you go on and busy yourself and I will see you later. I am going to help your Papa with some things in his study. He sure is looking healthier these days."

"Okay. I will see you later. I already got my horse ready. I will be home later, before dark."

Faith was taking her time riding into town. She felt like she was truly seeing everything for the first time. The sky seemed bluer; the grass greener. She was simply happy. She did not ever remember being this happy. She was thinking of Vayne on the seas wondering if he was thinking of her. She imagined that he was. She reached and felt her ring on her finger and smiled. She was going to be Mrs. Vayne Lafitte. She was smiling to herself when she had the sensation that she was being watched. She stopped for a minute and looked around. She did not see anyone.

Faith got to the bookstore and Ms. Alma was there as usual.

"Hello Ms. Alma. I wanted to come in and help you get chores done around here."

Alma looked at Faith and smiled, "You trying to pass the time until Vayne gets back in town, huh?"

"You know me well Ms. Alma."

Alma reached over and put her arms around Faith, "I am so glad you are going to be my family. You and Vayne both deserve happiness."

Faith smiled, "Me too."

Faith helped Ms. Alma in the store most of the day and part of the evening. "I better head back home. I told Maw Sally I would be back before dark. I do not want her and Papa to be worried."

"You head back now and be careful dear. I am fixing to close here and go home myself."

Faith left and headed back home. The plantation was not far from town, but it was darker than Faith realized. She felt a little uneasy. Halfway home Faith got the same sensation she did earlier. She felt as if she was being watched. She shook it off, "You're being paranoid," she told herself aloud. She nudged her horse to go faster. She bent down to go under a branch over the road when her horse pitched, and she was snatched from behind off the horse. She hit the ground with a thud. Faith felt the air leave her lungs. She laid on the ground for a minute to catch her breath. As she got up, she felt a kick in her ribs. Louis was standing over her. Faith felt fear rip through her.

"Hello cousin Faith," she heard Louis say just as he kicked her in the ribs again. Faith felt like she had been struck with a hammer. She could not scream or speak. The pain was excruciating.

"Remember me." he said through gritted teeth.

Faith saw his face and knew that she had never seen such rage and hatred from anyone in her life. She had also never seen her cousin like this. He was a mad man. There was no turning back for him now. She knew that. He was going to kill her.

"Louis, where have..." Faith did not even get the question out before another kick came, this time into her lower back. Faith felt pain rip though her. She would not give him the satisfaction of hearing her make a sound.

Faith gritted her teeth, "How are you cousin?"

With this, Louis grabbed her hair, picked her up from the ground, and jerked her up into his face, "How am I? You know how I am. I know how you are going to be when I am done with you," he pushed his mouth to hers and she bit him. He screamed out in pain. He tasted the blood. Faith spit his own blood into his face. She ran, but he still had his hand in her hair, and he snatched her back.

"Where do you think you're going bitch?" He spat at her. "I am not done with you yet. We have a lot of business to take care of," he let go of her hair and grabbed her arm.

Faith wanted to scream and cry, but she would not give in. She would not let him see her break, "Louis, what do you want? It is over. You will never get Edwards Plantation or Edwards Banking."

"Oh, that does not matter anymore. Your father loves you more than he loves that bank or house. I am taking the thing he loves most in this world. You," he said.

"You know that you will never get away with this. You will be caught and hanged," she spat at him.

"Don't you get it? I do not care about any of that anymore. I have lost everything. I have nothing more to lose. I will make you and Uncle pay," he said.

"Pay for what? What are we paying for? What did we do to you?" Faith yelled at him.

Louis looked at her and his face changed, "My mother saw through me. Even as a child, she tried to teach me the right way. When she saw that I had killed the kitten, she talked to me and told me that we should not hurt others. She found out I drowned a puppy, she still tried to talk to me and tell me that was not nice. She eventually stopped caring. She eventually said that I was naughty, and she would have to send me away. She said that if my father had not died, then maybe I would not be the way that I am. Don't you see Faith, I had to stop mother from sending me away."

Faith felt bile raise to her throat. She knew what he was fixing to say, but she did not want to hear it. She shook her head.

"I went into her room that night. I knew it was the perfect time because she had not been feeling well. So, I went into her room after everyone was asleep. I placed my hand over her nose and mouth and kept it there until she stopped breathing. I laid with her for a while until it was dawn. I then crept back to my room and got into bed. Don't you see Faith? I get what I want. I always get what I want."

Louis grabbed her hand and brought it to his lips. His kissed her hand. His face changed when he felt the ring on her left hand. He knew what it was. Faith could tell by his face. Faith felt her blood run cold as she looked up at him.

"I see that a lot has happened since I left. You and your pirate prince plan on wedding?"

His laugh made her hair stand on end. "Do you really think that I would ever let that happen?"

"There is nothing you can do to stop it cousin. You do not control my life or me. You are sick. Let me get you help," Faith said calmly.

"Get me help! There is no help that I need. The only help that I need is to make you and Uncle pay. I will take you Faith, but this is going to be slow and painful for you. I will have every inch of you and when I am done, your pirate will not want anything to do with you," he hissed.

Faith wanted to claw his eyes out. For a moment, she almost let him get to her, but she would never let Louis know that what he said frightened her. As kids, he used to bully her, but not now, not anymore. She tilted her head stubbornly and said, "He has already had me. Don't you see? I gave myself to him in every way possible, cousin. You are too late. He beat you to it."

As the words left her mouth, she took a blow to the side of her head, and she felt the darkness take over. She floated down slowly and saw Vayne's face and she sunk deeper into oblivion. She tried to cry out, but no words would come. All faded black.

Chapter 18
The Storm

Vayne cursed as he saw the storm clouds start to come into view in the distance. *Damn Paddy and his bones,* he thought. "All hands ahoy," Vayne yelled to the men. "You know we have a storm coming and we need to tie down all the barrels abaft," he pointed to the back area of the boat.

"Paddy, you old Seadog! You and your bones were right again!"

"Aye. Did not want to be right this time, but me bones never lie."

"Check the ballast in the hold as well. We need to make sure she stays balanced," Vayne said.

"Aye."

As Vayne was walking to the stem of the ship to take a closer look at the clouds, he got that sinking feeling again. Like something was wrong. He had been through storms before. He briefly thought of Faith and pushed the thought out of his mind. She was safe on land. He could not let his mind get the better of him.

"Men, get the storm sails up. We are going to ride this and use the momentum of the winds to push us further faster. I need all hands. This may be a rough one," he said sternly to his men.

Lightning crackled and boomed in the distance. The men were able to keep up with how far the lightning was by the sound of the thunder. The rain started to come in and the wind picked up. It was dark as the rain pounded the deck of the ship and the men. So far, the waves had not been more than what they were used too. Vayne felt confident they would ride this storm out and get through it with minimum damage.

He would keep the ship moving into the waves and use the wind in the sails to get enough speed to move over and into the waves. He just hoped the waves stayed at minimum level.

The seas were rough. The waves crashed over the side of the ship several times and sent the men slipping and bumping dangerously toward the edge. They tied ropes to themselves eventually to keep them stable. The rigging snapped, and it took three men to get it under control. The men fared well except for some cuts and bruises. They knew that it could have been much worse.

They rode out the storm over night with minimum damage to the ship and all the cargo accounted for. They took shifts the next day getting everything back in order and kept moving forward toward the island. Vayne did not know how much time they lost in the storm. They could not be more than a few hours off course. The wind was in their sails. He just knew he needed to get this cargo delivered and get back home. He had a feeling he needed to be back home.

They reached Isla de Cedros the following day. As he neared the island, he heard the familiar sound of the children running and yelling his name on the beach. He saw the woman come out of the woods and walk toward the shoreline. He could see their usual baskets used to gather clams around them. The fish were plentiful in this area, however, since the hurricane, they can only cast from the shoreline until they get the boats replenished. The storm also caused the island to change shape and the villagers are still trying to learn the area again.

Vayne threw anchor and lowered the planks. The men began to unload the cargo. Paddy tapped Vayne on the shoulder, "Sir, we got a problem. We got repairs that need to be done before we set sail to go back home. We found some loose planks and the some of the sails need to be repaired. I can repair the sails meself. It won't take more than a day or two and isn't anything we can't handle."

"It has to be done. You and the men get on it and I will help get the cargo unloaded. The sooner it is taken care of the better," Vayne walked away and started unloading the ship.

Vayne normally loved being here. He loved the people and their rituals. This time was different. This time he could not wait to leave and go back to the mainland. The only way he would ever enjoy this island again was when Faith could come with him. He did not like this ocean between them, especially when he did not know where Louis was. He just felt the need to go home.

Chapter 19
Missing

Maw Sally and John Edwards were pacing. It was after dark, and Faith had not made it back home yet. Ms. Alma said she had left the store before dark headed home. John knew instantly something was wrong when her horse showed up at home without her. He went out, searched, and found no sign of Faith.

"Where could she be?" John said as he ran his fingers through his hair.

"I suspect Louis has her," Maw Sally said.

John also suspected Louis had her. He prayed he was wrong. "I think you may be right Maw Sally. I do not know where to even begin to look for her."

"If he hurts one hair on that child's head, I see him dead," Maw Sally hissed.

John was sick with worry. He knew what Louis was capable of. He wished Vayne were here. He may know where to start. "I am going to go over to Trent's house and see if she may be over there. It is a long shot. But worth a try."

John arrived at Trent and Daisy's and knocked on the door. Trent came to the door, "Mr. Edwards is everything okay? Come in."

"I am afraid it is not. I was coming here to see if Faith was with you. Her horse showed up to the house without her. She was coming back home from town and she never made it." John just sat down in a chair feeling defeated.

Daisy walked over to him, "Do you think Louis has her?"

Louis looked up, "Yes. Yes, I do."

Daisy gasped. She knew all too well, what Louis was capable of. "Trent what are we going to do?"

"I do not know. Vayne will not be back for a day or so. I cannot wait on him to start looking for her. I will do some riding and see what I can find. Mr. Edwards, do you mind if Daisy rides to your place with you? I do not want to leave her here by herself."

"Of course not, I will take her with me. Do you have the carriage hitched up? If so, we can take that back to my place."

"Yes, we do. Daisy pack a bag. You may be there a few days," Trent kissed Daisy goodbye and rode off.

Trent felt in his gut that Faith was in big trouble. After witnessing, what Louis was in the midst of doing to the woman when he interrupted him, and after what he did to Daisy, he knew he had to try his best to find Faith and fast. He could only imagine what Vayne would do when he found out. He went first to the back of the bank where the makeshift office was where he took the paperwork. No one was there. *Dammit*, he thought.

Trent rode through town, it was late, and the town was dead silent. He rode down by the creek and up on the hill, where Vayne had killed Al and left him weeks before. He knew that they could have gone any direction. Damn! He wished his best friend were here. Trent felt responsible. He was supposed to look out for Faith as his friend would have been looking out for Daisy. Dammit to hell. He searched half the night and did not find her. He went the plantation to talk to the family to see if they could think of anywhere, he might have taken her.

Chapter 20
Hell

Faith woke up and felt the pain instantly. She knew that her ribs were broken. She was not sure how her face looked. She imagined she looked a mess. The room was pitch black. She had no clue where she was. She pressed her ear against the wall and could not hear any noise. It was quiet. She was barefoot. She panicked and felt her hand and had a rush of relief when she felt her ring. She heard rustling at the door. She backed against the wall.

"Hello Cousin. I thought I heard something rustling around," Louis walked in with a lantern. She could see his face as he smiled at her.

"Where am I?"

"You are where you should be. In a dark hole where you belong. No one will ever find you."

Faith kept her voice level. She stood and picked her chin up. She would not let him see her weak. "We are where you feel more comfortable. In a hole. Where you belong," she hissed.

Louis laughed, "You try to act so strong. You do not fool me, Faith. I know that you are weak. I know that you are scared, and I know that you want your papa."

Faith did not say a word. She just stared at him. She thought, *he is right. I am scared and I do want my papa, but he was wrong about one thing. I am not weak.*

"What's wrong Faith? Cat got your tongue?" Louis smirked.

She still said nothing.

"What? You got nothing to say now. You were so chatty before."

He walked over to her, bent down, picked her hand up, and looked at her ring. "I am going to let you keep your ring on. So that way when I take you, and I will, you can think of your precious Vayne and know that it is me taking you instead of him."

Faith felt her blood run cold. She was truly terrified. She knew he could do whatever he wanted to her. She knew that he could torture her forever and there was nothing she could do.

"Do what you must Louis. As I told you before, Vayne beat you to it. He took me first. Was that not what appealed to you? That I was a virgin. I saw you when we were kids taking sneak peeks at me when I was in the bath or changing. Do you think I do not know that you killed my kitten? It was because you could not do what you wanted to do to me? I know you better than you know yourself. So go ahead and take me now. Here! Come on! Do it now!" she screamed at him.

Louis did not know how to feel. She was right. Her appeal was that he wanted to take her. He wanted to be her first and the first man to touch her. The first man to teach her what being a woman was all about. That was supposed to be him.

He walked over to her, "Stand up!"

Faith was scared but knew she would endure what she had too. She stood up in front of him and leveled her breathing.

"Turn around," he said.

She turned around. He grabbed her hands, pulled them behind her back, and tied them. He turned her back around to face him. He leaned down and suckled her breast through her shirt. She did not make a noise. She knew he wanted her to, even if it was in fear. He bit her. She did not make a noise; she just looked at the ceiling. She remembered the day that she first met Vayne. She remembered walking along the creek bank holding his hand. She was remembering their first kiss when she felt a slap across her face.

Louis was staring at her, "You are just going to stand there. Stand there and act like it does not affect you in the least?" He shoved her so hard that she hit the wall and banged her head.

Faith started laughing. She laughed so hard that she could barely contain herself, "Yes Louis. I will stand here, lay here and you do whatever it is you want to do to me, and I will never make a sound," she said through giggles.

"You have lost your mind," Louis said.

Faith was laughing, "Yes. I have. I will never let you win. Don't you see? You are a joke, Louis! A walking, talking joke!"

Louis walked over and punched her in the stomach and then when she doubled over, he kneed her in the face. Faith continued to laugh until he decided he could not take it anymore. When he left, Faith's laughter turned into sobs. She cried for her. She cried for her mother. She cried for Vayne. She cried for Ebony. She cried for Maw Sally. Everything was running through her thoughts, and she just felt broken.

Faith was lying on the floor when she felt a cool sensation on her head. It was the feeling of someone stroking her hair. She saw a beautiful glow and felt a calmness wash over her. She raised her eyes and knew instantly that Ebony was comforting her. Maw Sally was right. Vayne looked just like her. The eyes, the hair, the face, and lips. Faith knew that she was being looked after. She also knew that this could be the end for her.

As Ebony started to fade away, Faith reached out and said, "Please don't leave me."

Faith heard, "Never my daughter. You and my son will fulfill my legacy. Stay strong in faith."

Faith felt a calmness wash over here. She fell into a peaceful slumber.

Chapter 21
Message

Vayne was not in a good mood and his crew knew it. They had repaired the planks and sails on the ship and finally set sail. He was ready to get home. It would take two to three days to get back to the mainland. He felt something was wrong. He could not put his finger on it, but he knew something was off. "I am going below deck. Do not disturb me," Vayne barked to the crew.

"Aye," Paddy said.

The crew knew their Captain was out of sorts today. That much was obvious. They suspected it was to do with a certain lady, but none would dare say it.

Vayne made his way to his cabin, took off his clothes, and got into his bed. He could not figure out why he was so angry. He had been short with his men today and plain nasty to everyone. He figured it was best to just go to bed and sleep it off. He laid there for a while and felt the ship rocking back and forth and it lulled him to sleep. He dreamt of Faith and their first kiss, the first day they met. He dreamed he was looking at her and her face started to change. He saw blood on her mouth and her face was bruised. This startled him awake. He did not know how long he had been asleep. He was breathing hard and sat up for a minute and then went back to bed. As he lay there, he felt a cold sensation. He saw a beautiful light out of the corner of his eye. He looked to his left and saw his mother. She was smiling at him. He felt tears escape from the corner of his eyes.

"Mother?" he whispered.

She nodded and only smiled.

Vayne knew when he saw her that this meant she was not alive. He was not sad, but enlightened.

"Mother, I have missed you," he said.

She smiled, "You must get home my son. She needs you."

"Mother who needs me? Faith?"

She nodded and smiled. She started to fade.

"Please don't leave me Mother."

He heard her say, "Never my son. You and she will fulfill my legacy. Stay strong in faith."

Vayne went back to sleep. It was not peaceful. He would not be peaceful until he was back with Faith.

Chapter 22
Searching

Trent had searched everywhere. He was in a panic and did not know what else to do. Vayne was due back any day now. Trent had ridden by the sea every couple of hours to see if he saw the ship coming in. Daisy was beside herself. They were staying at with the Edwards until they got Faith home. Ms. Alma was also at the plantation, helping Maw Sally anyway she could.

"I need that child home," Maw Sally said dabbing at her eyes with her apron.

"I know me too," Ms. Alma said.

John Edwards was pacing. He was beside himself with worry. He had not slept since she went missing and had not stopped looking. He was out of ideas on where to look. He just did not know where they could be.

"I don't know what else to do. I have looked everywhere that I know to look," John said.

"I am going to ride back over and see if Vayne is back yet," Trent said.

Trent mounted his horse and took off to the shore. As he neared the shoreline, he caught site of the sails of The Lady Ebony. He sped up and was waiting on the shoreline when the ship made it to dock. Vayne climbed down off the ship and waked toward his friend. He could tell by the look on Trent's face something was wrong.

"What's wrong Trent?"

Trent did not know what to do say, "It is Faith. She is gone."

"What do you mean gone? How can she be gone? She would never just leave," Vayne snapped.

"I know she would not. We think Louis has her. We have searched high and low, and we are out of options. We do not know where else to look," Trent said.

Vayne felt his blood run cold. He knew in his gut that Louis had her. He had felt that something was wrong since he left and knew that is why his mother visited him.

Vayne and Trent rode together back to the plantation. As Vayne walked into the door, everyone was dead silent.

"Do you have any idea where he could be with her? Is there anywhere of which you have not thought? A barn, stable, anywhere?" Vayne Asked.

John said, "I have searched everywhere I know to search. I do not know what to do. I want my daughter home."

Vayne sat down beside John. "There must be one place no one has thought of. A place that he would have gone. I would bet it is not far from here. He is out for revenge, so he would not have gone far."

"It has too somewhere familiar for him. He has been a creature of habit since he was a small child. He was a sick boy just as he is a sick man. I saw it over the years, and I just sat by quietly and watched. I knew he would do something crazy one day, but I just never thought it would include my Faith. His poor mama knew it too. She did not know what to do with that child. He needs to be put out of his own misery," Maw Sally said.

Vayne gritted his teeth, "He will be put permanently out of his own misery when I get my hands on him."

Vayne could feel his insides twisting with worry, "Everyone sit down, and let's think. We must think of anywhere nearby that he used to visit. We need to check under every rock. He is here somewhere."

Everyone pulled up a chair at the table and began to discuss Louis, his habits, and his childhood playgrounds where he used to hang out.

Chapter 23
Fighting Back

Faith woke up, although sore, battered, and bruised; she knew that she had to fight back. It was cold and damp. There was a little sunlight coming from somewhere. Just light enough to illuminate where she could focus her eyes. She looked around, she did not notice last night, but the walls looked like rock. She was in some sort of cave. Her hands were bound behind her back. She searched frantically looking for something to help get her loose or to protect herself with.

Faith remembered that she had hit her head on something sharp when knocked into the wall. She slid her hands around and felt a piece of rock. She backed up to the rock and rubbed the rope up and down on the side of the rock. It started to get hot on her hand. She rubbed even harder, and she felt the ropes give. She smiled to herself and felt a renewed sense of hope.

She walked around to see if she could find anything to protect herself. She realized when he came into the cave that she did not hear a door but something scrape. She ran over to where the opening should be, and she could feel raw wood. She pushed, pushed, and could not get it to budge.

"Damn!" she swore aloud.

There was nothing she found to use as a weapon, "I will just have to improvise," she mumbled.

She heard him coming. She rushed to where she was laying earlier and put her hands back behind her back as if they were still bound.

"Hello Cousin," Louis cooed.

"Wow you look atrocious," he laughed.

"You need a bath. What do you think?" he asked.

"I think I would rather stink."

"Still got your spunk, I see. I will break your spirit eventually and make you beg me to hurt you," he said.

"That will never happen Louis. I promise you that."

"Oh, we shall see. Are you hungry?" Louis asked.

"No."

"Oh, c'mon you have to eat something. You would not want to shrivel up and die in here, would you?"

"Where am I anyway?" Faith asked.

"You are at one of my favorite places," he said.

"What favorite place?"

"Do you remember the falls? The falls in the woods, behind the planation."

She shook her head.

"Oh, c'mon. You remember. Some folks call them Ebony Falls, because of the color of the rocks. I know you remember. We played here as kids. You always hid from me. I tried to kiss you in the water fall and you told on me."

Faith suddenly remembered. This is the place where he tried to kiss her for the first time, and she told on him. He got mad and drowned her kitten. She remembered. How could she ever have forgotten that? This is where it all started. It made sense now.

"Oh, I see. So, you want to give me a bath so you can drown me as you did my kitten. Is that it Louis? You do not get your way, so you just kill whatever it is to hurt the other person. You are going to drown me to hurt papa. Am I right?"

"Now you're catching on," he said.

Faith had a million thoughts running through her head. She had to figure a way to get outside. She knew the way back to the house. If only she could just get outside.

"Louis?" she called his name.

"Yes Faith."

"I am ready to take my bath now. Will you take me outside to take my bath?" She was trying to stay calm. Give him what he wants. She just needed to get outside. That was her only chance.

"I do not know. You said you would rather be dirty," he said.

"I was wrong Louis. I was wrong about everything. I think I may have even been wrong about you. I am so sorry. I should have been nicer to you. I should have let you kiss me under the waterfalls. I mean, what would it have hurt?" Faith was trying her best to convince him to take her outside.

"Why the change of heart now?" he asked.

"Because you bringing it up now just shows me how cruel I was. It was my fault. I should have just let you have your way with me. I deserve to be punished Louis. I deserve it. I remember you like to cleanse things. I think you should take me outside to the falls and cleanse me as you cleansed the kitten. Please Louis I am begging you," Faith insisted.

"I do not trust you. You are trying to trick me," he said.

"No. I am done with games Louis. I learned from you; it is not worth it."

Louis walked over to her. Her stomach lurched in fear. She knew she had to get outside. He touched her breast, and he was watching her. He was staring at her; she knew that he was trying to get a reaction from her. She was not sure what to do. She did not know what would set him off or what would make him stay calm.

"How does that feel cousin? Do you like me touching you?" he asked.

Faith could not bring herself to say yes, "I think I would like it better after a bath when I am clean. Can you please give me a bath? I am begging you. I want you to bathe me."

Louis just stared at her. She could not read his mind. She did not know what his next move would be. He stared at her for what seemed like hours, but she knew it was mere seconds.

"Okay, I think I can manage giving you a bath. I hope you like it rough though."

"Maybe you need to go ahead and open the entrance, since I am tied up and all and make it easier for yourself."

"Cousin, you are looking out for me. That is good," he said.

Faith held her breath as he walked over to the entrance and slid the covering to one side. He got her by the arm, she kept her arms firmly behind her. She needed to make sure he showed her the way out before he realized she was not tied up. He led her down a cave. It was not a deep cave, but just back enough it would be hard to spot if you did not know it was there. It was level with the ground but just left of the falls. Faith's heart starting racing as she saw the grass through the entrance.

"Louis, thank you for walking me out here and agreeing to do this. I really appreciate it."

Before he could answer her, she hit him from behind, knocked him down, and took off running. She could hear her behind him. Her heart was racing. She knew that she just needed to get to the house. She had to get to the house. She needed to get home. She would be safe there. She was afraid to look back in fear that he would grab her. She was terrified he would catch her before she got home. Faith ran and as she saw the back of the house come into view, she started screaming. She was still screaming when she pounced up the steps and fell hard on the porch. She was screaming and fighting. Someone was on top of her on the porch. She was hitting and pounding with her eyes shut. She could not breathe.

"Faith it's me Vayne," He knew from her screams she did not know it was him and did not realize she was safe. She was fighting him out of fear.

He tried again, as he was sitting on the porch with her cradled in his lap, "Faith. Baby it is me. It's Vayne. You are safe. Please. It is me."

He felt her ease up fighting. He held her and felt her start to calm down. When she looked up at him and he saw her bruised face, the cuts, the bruised arms, he almost lost it, but he held it together.

She looked up into his face and he saw the moment she realized it was him. She reached up and touched his face, traced his jawline, touched his lips.

"It's you?" she asked lightly.

"Yes, Faith. It's me. You're safe now."

She ran her hands down his arms and over his back. Around his neck and touched his face again, "Please don't leave me?" she asked.

He reached down and touched her bruised face, "I will never leave you again."

He picked her up and carried her upstairs to her room.

The others knew it was time to leave them alone.

Chapter 24
The Bath

As Vayne walked through the screen door, carrying Faith, he motioned to Maw Sally to heat some water. She went to fetch the water to put it on to heat. Vayne climbed the stairs and went into Faith's room. He gently laid her on the bed. He knelt beside the bed and touched her face gently. "I am going to take your dress off. Is that okay?" he asked.

She nodded. Her hands were trembling. He took her hands into his and rubbed them.

"It is okay. I am here now. You are safe and I will not leave your side. I promise."

He gently undid the buttons on her dress. He slid the dress off and had to hold his breath when he saw the bruises on her shoulders. As he pulled the dress down further, he saw the bite mark on her breast. He fought back tears. As he pulled the dress down to her waist, he saw the bruises around her ribs and stomach and his heart dropped. He knew that she had some internal injuries from the looks of it. He gently laid her back on the bed and finished undressing her. She was bruised down her thighs and legs and her feet were badly bruised and bleeding. He got a blanket and wrapped it around her.

"I am going to check your back. Is that okay?"

She nodded. Her back was battered but he could see those were superficial. As he thought about how badly she was hurt, his fear was what scars she would carry on the inside from what she had been through. He had to put that thought out of his head so he could focus on her.

"Faith, I am going to help you bathe. Is that okay?"

"Yes, she said," her voice sounded like a whisper. It reminded him of a wounded child.

Maw Sally entered the room with the steaming water and poured it into the tub. Maw Sally cringed when she saw the bruises and she just nodded at Vayne and left the room.

Vayne gently picked her up and eased her down into the bathtub of water. Her breath caught. He knew she was sore and was hurting. Vayne eased the cloth down into the water and gently caressed her. He knew he had to get her cleaned up so that he would assess her injuries closer. He needed to know what happened but knew that it would take time for her to open up. He feared the worst.

"Faith, I am going to wash your hair. I want to make sure that is okay with you. I will never do anything that you do not want me to. I need you to tell me. Okay?" he asked.

He gently eased her head back into the water and his hand touched her throat, she flinched. Vayne stopped, leaned down and said, "It is okay. Do you want me to stop?"

Faith looked up at him, "No. Thank you for helping me."

He rubbed her back, her ribs, which he could tell were broken. He rubbed her feet and legs. After he finished bathing her, he gently picked her up from the bath with ease and took her to the bed. He dried her hair and helped her to dress. He held her for a long time.

She looked up at him, "Thank you. I thought I would never see you again. I thought I was going to die."

"Faith, I am so sorry. I never should have left you here alone. I will never forgive myself for allowing this to happen to you."

Faith wrapped her arms around him, "Shhhhh, this is not your fault or my fault. There is only one person to blame."

Vayne cupped her face in his hands and looked into her eyes, "Did he..." he could not finish his sentence. A tear rolled down his cheek.

"No. He did not hurt me in that way."

Vayne was relieved he did not violate her in that manner. He knew that it would take a while, but she could heal from these wounds, and they may leave emotional scars but was relieved to know she was not violated in that way.

"Will you stay with me?" Faith asked.

"Of course, I will. You are stuck with me," he smiled.

Faith smiled, "I am glad to be stuck with you."

He laid back on the bed and she rested her head on his chest.

Faith propped herself up on her elbow, "I have something to tell you. You may not believe it. I saw your mother. I know that she approves of us. She was with me in the cave. She was looking out for me."

"I know. She came to me too. You are right. She does approve."

They both smiled. There was no more that needed to be said. Not on this day.

Chapter 25
Setting The Date

A few weeks had passed, and Louis was nowhere to be found. Everyone was on high alert. No one was ever left alone. Trent and Daisy were still at the plantation. Ms. Alma had gone home, and Vayne was in the guest room full time at the plantation. Faith was still a bit jumpy, but she was making progress, and the bruises were healing. Her ribs were wrapped secure but doing well.

"Child don't you go fetch no more water. I will get it for you if you need it," Maw Sally scolded.

"Grammy, do not go fetch no more water. I will get it for you if you need it," Vayne scolded.

All three of them laughed, "Vayne, I am one happy Grammy to have you home. I am even happier that you and Ms. Faith are together. Your mama would have been so proud," Maw Sally said.

"I know for a fact she is happy and approves," Vayne winked at Faith.

"Now ladies, what is the deal on this wedding you are supposed to be planning? I have not heard a word about it," He looked at Faith, "You do still want to marry me, right? Or are you tired of me yet?"

Faith popped him on the arm, "You know that is not true. I am going to get you hitched up. You are mine now," she laughed.

"Well, I am glad to hear it, because I want to get you all hitched up too. I do not want any prince charming coming through here snatching you up from me," he joked.

"I actually do have an idea and I wanted to talk to you about it," Faith said with a raised brow.

Vayne looked at Faith, "What's the idea?"

"I think we should have the wedding on The Lady Ebony," Faith said.

Vayne grinned, "Really? You would really want to do that?"

Faith clapped her hands together and squealed, "Yes, I think it would be great! We could do it all there. The ceremony, reception." She cleared her throat, "The honeymoon."

Vayne slapped his hands against his legs, "Well we got us a wedding venue and it is ready to go! Let's do it!"

Faith said, "How about we do it next Saturday?"

Vayne said, "I am free and don't have any plans and if I did, they would be with you, anyway."

Maw Sally sat there and was unusually quiet. Vayne and Faith looked at each other with raised brows, "Maw Sally is something wrong?" they asked.

"No. Something is just mighty right. Do you know what next Saturday is?" she asked.

"No ma'am, I don't. Do you Vayne?" Faith asked.

Vayne scratched his head, "No. I do not. What is next Saturday?"

"Child, next Saturday is my Ebony's birthday. I do not believe in coincidences. I believe in divine intervention. I think yawl done picked a fine day for your wedding and I know your sweet mama approves," Maw Sally said through tears.

Faith and Vayne wrapped their arms around each other and knew in that moment, all was as it should be.

Chapter 26
Ebony's Statue

Everyone on Edwards Plantation was in good spirits. They were planning the wedding; Daisy and Trent were expecting their first child. The days seemed longer, and the nights seemed shorter. It had been quiet, too quiet.

Vayne was watching Faith from a distance. He knew that she was on edge and looking over her shoulder. They both knew that eventually Louis would show up again. He had been hiding under a rock since all that happened. He was a slimy snake, could hide in the dark, and only come out when hungry. Vayne knew that it was only a matter of time. It sickened to him to know what he had put Faith through. Vayne knew that eventually; Louis would get what was coming to him.

"What are you thinking about?" Faith had walked up on the porch and Vayne was so deep in thought.

"I am thinking about us," he smiled and looked away.

Faith knew he was lying. He was thinking about the same thing she was. She understood because she did not want him to know it was on her mind constantly either. The nightmares were bad enough, but she could not shake it, even when awake.

"I will be glad when all this is over with. I will be glad when we can put that son of a bitch six foot under where he belongs," he said more to himself than to her, "He does not deserve to be walking around!"

Faith was wondering how long it would take him to blow. She has been waiting on his emotions to surface. He had been holding so much in for her. She knew he needed a release. She just sat silently and let him rant.

"It takes a coward to do something like this. To hurt people on purpose," he stood up and stomped down the steps, "I wish he was standing in front of me right now."

Faith eased up off the steps and walked over to him, "I am angry too. I feel like we are letting him control he and us is not even here. If we let him steal our joy, he wins."

"I know. You are right. I feel like he is winning right now. All I can think about is getting my hands on him. The thought of him laying his hands on you…"

Faith knew that there was nothing she could say or do right now to make him feel any better. She knew him well enough to know that she needed to let him vent. She was dealing with things in her own way too. She did not know how she would react on their honeymoon night. It made her nervous. She was not sure what he expected of her. She did not know if he would look at her the same, after what had happened. She was not sure what she was feeling, she just felt numb. They had not done more than hold hands since she got back from that nightmare. He had not even kissed her. Not like he used to before this happened. She felt so unsure of herself. She felt dirty.

Vayne was still ranting when he looked over and saw Faith looking out toward the creek. He knew that look. He could tell she was far away in her thoughts. It broke his heart to see her look like this. He knew she felt the need to be strong. He also knew that she needed him more than she would let on. He needed her more than she realized. He could not imagine what she had went through. He would never ask her. She would never know how much respect he had for her. He knew she was stronger than she appeared, and he did not doubt for a minute that she would be simply fine. He walked over and got her hand, "C'mon. Let us go inside. I am hungry and I smell whatever Grammy is cooking."

After supper, they all decided to go into the parlor and relax. As they were walking toward the parlor, Vayne felt Faith freeze. He heard the chuckle and then a blast. Vayne felt the bullet when it hit him and was on the floor in an instant and smelled gunpowder. As he tried to get up, he felt another sharp pain following another loud pop. He heard Faith scream and then blackness folded in around him.

Faith turned just in time to see Louis running at her with the gun out in front of him, as closed her eyes and waited for the shot, she heard a loud crash and then a thud. Faith was waiting on the blow, but when she opened her eyes, she saw Maw Sally standing over Louis and the statue that Vayne's mother had given as a gift all those years ago laying on top of him. Maw Sally bent down to check his pulse, "I said if you harmed one hair on that child's head, I was gonna getcha. Well. I gotcha."

Before Maw Sally got up from checking his pulse, she reached into the statue and pulled out some papers. She turned around and handed them to John Edwards, "Here are your original deeds. I hid them in the statute for safe keeping the night you gave them to me. I knew they would be safe there."

John Edwards could not speak. He took the papers, tucked them in his pocket, and fixed himself a whiskey.

Faith gathered herself enough to run over to Vayne. He was alive. Someone must fetch the doc. He has lost a lot of blood.

Trent had been standing outside when he heard the shot, "I will go and get him," he yelled over his shoulder, as he was running out the door.

Faith sat with his head cradled in her lap, "Please do not leave me. Please. We have only just gotten started. Please! God, No!" She begged.

Chapter 27
Moving Forward

The Lady Ebony was adorned, as she had never been before. There were white streamers strung from one side to the other. The crew had really outdone themselves. They cooked a feast of lamb, pork, fish, just to name a few. The wedding cake was enormous. It was in the center of the table. It was a masterpiece. As Faith walked toward the ship, the site astounded her.

Faith looked beautiful in her mother's white dress and long satin gloves. She wore her hair down, in all its red glory. She pulled the front back and fastened it loosely away from her face. She did not carry a bouquet. She had no need for one. She was beautiful all on her own. She wore an emerald necklace that was gifted to her by Maw Sally as something old. It was a simple necklace with one single stone, but she loved it. As Vayne looked down and saw her, she took his breath away. He could not hide his grin. It lit his entire face up.

As Faith was walking toward him, she could never imagine. He was wearing attire she had not seen before, and she loved it. He was wearing a white loose blouse, black tight breeches with black boots and a tricorn hat that quite become him. She had never witnessed him like this before and it made her heart skip a beat. Oh, she was ready to be his wife. She briefly thought of her what their honeymoon had in store and to her surprise, she was not scared, she was excited.

John Edwards was in awe of the two young people in front of him. They made a beautiful couple. He fought back tears as he performed the nuptials, "I now pronounce you husband and wife. You may kiss your bride" Vayne kissed his bride and the crew of the Lady Ebony cheered.

The festivities lasted into the early morning hours, however, the newlyweds snuck off early to his cabin quarters. As they made their way into the cabin, they found a surprise for them, courtesy of Trent and Daisy. They found food, candies, drinks, and they had placed rose petals in the bed. "I bet I know whose idea the rose petals were," Vayne grinned, "Daisy. Cause I know Trent is not smart enough to come up with that idea," he walked toward Faith. He wanted her so bad, but he was not sure how she would react to him. He did not want to scare her. He gently touched her face, "If you are not ready for this, it is okay," he said.

Faith eased toward him, "I am okay. I want this. I want you. I want all of you."

"I am not sure you are ready for all of me. I know that this is your first time and do not want to hurt you."

Faith put her head down and he put his finger under her chin so she would look at him, "What's wrong?"

"I just hope that what happened has not made you look at me differently."

"Yes, it does make me look at you differently," he sat down on the bed and pulled her down beside him, "It makes me love you even more. You are strong."

At that moment, Faith lost all her inhibitions. She wanted him like nothing she had ever wanted in her life. She wanted him to teach her how to be a lover. She wanted to learn from him. She stood up in front of him as he sat on the bed. She shyly let her wedding gown slide to the floor. He reached out and gently pulled her to him. She trembled as he reached for her. She feared disappointing him. Vayne could feel her shaking.

He eased her to him, "We do not have to rush anything. We can take our time. We have our whole lives," he kissed her and eased her down onto the bed. He wanted her to understand that there was nothing to fear. Making love was a beautiful thing.

As they kissed, caressed, and discovered one another they both began to figure out what the other liked. He kissed her face, her hands, and fingers. "I want you to close your eyes and let me love you. I want to take away your fears. I will never leave you. You are mine and I am yours forever," as he touched her again, he whispered in her ear, "I need you to tell me what you want and let me know when you are ready."

Faith pulled him closer on top of her, "I want you. I need you. Please. I am ready."

Faith tensed but only for a moment. As they melted into each other, they both understood that this was a fresh start to a new legacy.

EBONY'S LEGACY

Book 2: The Legacy Continues

Dawn Carr

Prologue

Vayne awoke startled. The last thing he remembered was being shot, the smell of gunpowder and Faith screaming. He turned his head in the bed and saw Faith asleep, holding his hand. He felt the pain in his shoulder where the bullet entered. He grunted and saw Faith stir.

"You are awake. I have been so worried about you," Faith leaned forward and kissed his hand.

"I will be fine. Is Louis dead?"

Faith shook her head, "No. He is alive."

"He will not be when I get my hands on him. He needs to be put down like the animal that he is."

Faith could see the anger boiling in his eyes. She knew that he meant every word. She felt the same way. She wanted Louis out of their life for good. She did not want to look over her shoulder and worry when he would come after them.

"I have something that I need to tell you. When the sheriff was taking him into town, after he shot you, he escaped."

"What do you mean escaped? He got away. How is that even possible?"

Faith shook her head, "I do not know. The Sheriff said that when he got to town and went to get him out of the covered wagon, the door was ajar, and he was gone."

Vayne was furious, "I have never seen a person have so many chances as him. He has luck wherever he goes."

"He should hang for what he's done," Vayne said, as he struggled to sit up.

Faith touched his face. "You need to rest now. We can worry about him later. You need your strength. We have a wedding to focus on. Remember?"

"Yes. I know. I just hate all this. I hate that he is still breathing," he said through clenched teeth.

"I know, but he does not control our happiness. He will get what is coming to him," Faith rubbed his hand.

Vayne shook his head, "He will hide, for a while, and then slither out, and attack and we will be ready for him. When I am up and strong enough, I am going to teach you ways to defend yourself so that the next time he comes after you, you will be ready for him."

Chapter 1
Voyage To Home

It had been three months since the wedding. Faith and Vayne were determined to spend as much time as possible on "The Lady Ebony" at sea. Faith loved being on the ship and her natural sea legs apparent. She had not been sick one time in the three months since they had set sail. Vayne loved watching her and the smile on her face let him know she was thoroughly enjoying it. He knew she would enjoy being on the sea as much as she would enjoy being on land at home. Faith has not really thought about where they would settle. She was enjoying this adventure at sea.

Faith was watching Vayne as he steered the ship into a small cove. She saw the muscles ripple in his taunt arms and strong legs. Her heart gave a little skip. *This is my beautiful husband.* She smiled to herself, and her heart swelled with pride. In the past three months, she had learned several things, but the one that astounded her, was he only had eyes for her and that was very apparent in the way he made love to her? He was right when he told her; there was no need to be afraid. Boy, was he right. She loved every minute. She loved feeling his touch on her skin. She had never felt safer than when she was in his arms. These thoughts made her grow hot. She had to brush them off and put them to the back of her mind, for now.

Vayne dropped anchor and informed his men they could go ashore. They were going to be here for the night. He wanted some alone time with his bride. He felt himself stir as he watched her. He knew that this woman would never realize just how much he loved her. She stirred things inside him that no other woman had ever touched. He had worried, after all that happened with Louis, if she would be able to trust a man. She had surprised him on their wedding night and even now. She was so open with him. She trusted him. He admired how strong she was. Even now, she was strong, knowing that Louis escaped. He was still out there. How he had slipped from the sheriff's clutches, was beyond any of them. This was one reason they decided to go on a sea voyage. To get away, so that they knew, he would not be able to rear his ugly head.

Vayne walked up behind Faith and wrapped his arms around her, "Are you ready to go below? I have wanted you all day long."

Faith smiled, "I sure am. The question is, are you ready?"

He groaned and picked her up and made their way below deck. She wrapped her arms around his neck and kissed him. "I love you so much."

Vayne smiled, "I love you back. ou will never realize just how much."

"You will just have to show me," She purred.

"Woman you don't know what you do to me. I used to be very satisfied just hanging out with my men and having a drink with Trent. Now I just want to spend all my time with you."

Faith smiled, "Maybe if you had not taught me so well, you would not be so content."

"You have taught me a few things yourself," he laughed.

He sat her gently down to her feet when they reached his quarters. She watched him as she unbuttoned her dress. She did not blink. She locked his gaze. As she did this, he walked toward her, "Let me help you with that, Mrs. Lafitte."

She turned around so he could reach her corset in the back. As he slowly undid her corset, he licked the side of her neck. He knew exactly what she liked. She turned toward him and slid her arms around his neck; she knew what he liked also. He groaned and picked her up and carried her to the bed. They explored every inch of each other, as they always did.

Afterwards, as they lay entangled, Faith was unusually quiet. Vayne rolled over onto his stomach so he could look at her. "What's wrong?"

She looked over at him, "It has been three months, and I am not pregnant. Do you think something is wrong with me?"

"No. I don't think anything is wrong, I think that it will happen when the time is right." He bent down and kissed her. It had crossed his mind a few times. He honestly thought she would be with child by now. However, they had their entire lives ahead of them. They both wanted a child so much. It would happen eventually. At least, he hoped it would.

"I hope you are right. Daisy got pregnant so quickly, I thought for sure we would as well. I want to give you a son."

Vayne smiled, "I want a daughter. I want her to look just like you. Don't you fret. We will get our baby. It just takes time."

She smiled, "While we are waiting, why don't we get busy and keep practicing?"

"Yes Ma'am. Practice makes perfect," he obliged his wife.

Chapter 2
Finding Home

The next day, Vayne and Faith decided they wanted to go and explore the island. They departed from the ship and made their way. They held hands as they walked the shoreline. Faith took in the sights. There were beautiful flowers along the wood line by the forest. She did not know the names of them, but they were beautiful. There were big flowers with a color that reminded her of the inside of a watermelon and the outer flower was a bright yellow. There were purple flowers that made her want to reach out and touch them, which she did. The silkiness of the flower was soft against her fingers. It was a beautiful site. She took off her shoes so that she could feel her toes in the sand.

"You will need to put those back on before we go into the trees," Vayne warned her.

"Where are we going?" she asked puzzled.

"To explore and see what this place has to offer."

Faith was amazed at these beautiful surroundings. She had never been out of Edwardstown. She had never seen the sights of this tropical place. She had seen the coast of course, but it was nothing like this magical place. She glanced back toward the ship and noticed the clear emerald coastline. The water was clear like the crystal on the chandelier back at the plantation. It astounded her. The beauty of it all was breathtaking.

"I wonder if anyone has ever been to this island," pondered aloud.

"I have." Vayne grinned.

Faith smiled, "I should have known."

"I am full of surprises my dear wife. This is one of my favorite places. Mother's tribe claimed this land years ago. They moved on a while ago, however, I intended to keep it. The wildlife and sea life are plentiful here."

"You intended to keep it? That is past tense. Do you not want to keep it now?"

"That depends on you, Faith. We are a team now. We decide together on how we want to live and grow. We are a family." He looked at her and smiled.

"Is it possible to keep it? How do we know that no one else has claimed it?"

"President Andrew Jackson protected our rights to the land back on the mainland. When he passed the "Removal Act," however, this land is not on U. S. soil and is not a territory. It is a free game. I am not even sure anyone else knows this island is here." Vayne smiled.

"We better get to exploring. I want to see more of Lafitte Island," Faith said as she linked her fingers through his.

Vayne led Faith into the edge of the woods, and she could see that there was a worn path. He had obviously been down this path many times. They walked for what seems like minutes and never said a word. As they came to the end of the path, a clearing opened, and it took Faith's breath away. It was a beautiful cottage. It was not huge, like the plantation, but it was not tiny either. On the front there was a porch made of stone that was three to four feet high. It ran the entire length of the house. The steps to the porch were made of stone. The roof looked as if it was made from straw and mud. Faith could see that this house had been here quite a while. The site astounded her. You would never know that a huge field was on this island, let alone, a beautiful cottage. She noticed the window boxes on the front windows and knew that they were recently added, due to the contrast of the wood. Faith looked up at Vayne, "Is this your house?"

He smiled, "No. It is our house. If you like it."

As they walked up the steps toward the door, she immediately felt like she was at home. It was a feeling that she never expected to feel. It overwhelmed her as she fought back tears. The front door was mahogany and the top arched. It reminded her of something whimsical out of a children's book. Vayne reached and opened the door, and the inside took her by surprise. It was so quaint and softer than she would have thought. He stood back and watched her as she looked around. Her smile said it all.

There was a staircase, to the right of the room, which led to a loft. Straight ahead was a kitchen. It had a wood burning stove in the corner and a rectangular shaped table in the center and was open to the rest of the house. There was a sink on the wall with a window overlooking the backyard. To the left was the living room and on the wall was a stone fireplace that reached from floor to ceiling. It was a magnificent site. The stone was a mixture of white, browns and blacks. Faith had never seen a stone like this before. In front of and facing, the fireplace was a Victorian carved beige sofa with mahogany wood legs. To the left of that was a sideboard of mahogany with ornate pulls. The furnishings were nice but modest. The décor suited Faith. She liked things simple. She came from a family of wealth, but those things never mattered to her. Simplicity was her comfort.

"Vayne this is beautiful. I love it. How long have you had this place?" she asked.

"When I found this place years ago, it was only a shell. I did all the work on the inside. The bones were already here, but it was just a blank space. I dug the stones for the fireplace myself and brought them here on the ship. This entire island was abandoned years before we found it. The rest of the grounds are a work in progress. I love this house, but you must know, I have never lived in it. When we move into this house, it will be a first for both of us. I have another place to show you once you finish exploring the house."

He led her up the stairs by the hand. As they got the top of the stairs, the entire top floor opened. There were two small rooms to the right and one spacious room to the left. In the middle was a study with a desk. Faith smiled to herself. She knew that this was big enough to start a family. All the rooms were on the top floor in the loft. He walked her to the left into the master suite. There was a huge feather stuffed bed and a fireplace also.

"Mr. Lafitte, this is beautiful. Are you trying to get me into bed?"

"I might be," he wrapped his arms around her and walked her backward toward the bed. He leaned down and kissed her lightly on the forehead. "I am glad you like this place. I was hoping you would."

"I am happy as long as I am with you."

"If am correct, there are two other rooms upstairs?" she asked.

Vayne smiled, "You are correct."

"So that means we have enough room to start a family, when we are ready."

"Again, you are correct."

Faith giggled and wrapped her arms around his neck. She was not sure why she was so ready to start a family. She had never thought much about it until she married him. Now it was all she could think about. She wanted to carry a part of him inside of her.

"I have something I want to show you," Vayne took her hand. He led her out the back door, there field was flat and looked out over the ocean from high bluffs the sight of it astounded her. She followed Vayne as he led her on a rock path toward a small grove of trees. As they entered the trees, a covered path opened to a magnificent sight. Her breath caught in her throat as she saw this beautiful lighthouse appear.

"Oh, that is beautiful. I have never seen one before, except in books," she said.

Vayne smiled, "This is my favorite place on the island. It was bad shape when we got here. It will always be a work in progress to keep it up and going."

The lighthouse was tall with a tower at the top. The tower had glass that enclosed the lantern room. The tower itself, constructed from wood and masonry. The Vayne opened the door, and they entered the service room. To the left were lamp chimneys, which were exceptionally clean, despite the age of the tower. In the middle of the tower were spiral stairs. She followed Vayne up the stairs and at the top; it opened to the windows. The view of the ocean was stunning. It made Faith feel tiny as she looked out over the horizon.

"We will not go any further than here, because the next level is the catwalk, and I do not want you to go up there. I will manage that part. I have made myself the lighthouse keeper. When we have a son, I will hand that job down to him," Vayne said looking out over the ocean.

Faith was smiling as she looked out over the ocean, "This place feels like a sanctuary. It feels safe and I am proud to call this land my home."

"I have sat here often and just sat quietly and listened. Listening to the waves and listened to myself," he said.

Faith did not need to ask any questions; she understood him completely. She could relate to the need for solitude.

They stood there for a while watched the ocean and listened to the sounds. The smells of the salt air hit her nostrils despite the glass. It felt clean and refreshing. The sea gulls were in full flight dipping in and out of the water. Up and down, they would dip until they caught whatever prey they were after. He took her hand, "Let us go home. I am ready to start this new life."

As they wound down the stairs and headed to leave the lighthouse, Faith felt a chill come across her neck. She stopped in mid-step. He did not notice her pause, walked on to the door, and opened it. She had no clue what that feeling was. Chills ran up her back and down her arms. She was sensing something but could not put her finger on it. Faith was learning, as she got older, that she had a special gift and was learning to listen to her gift, some called it a sixth sense.

Chapter 3
That same day, Back in Edwardstown

Maw Sally was pitter-pattering around the kitchen humming to herself. She was lost in thought. She was angry and in awe at the same time at how Louis could have managed to get away. *How does a scoundrel like that have so many lives and keeps getting away? Should have killed that low life when I had the chance. I was standing over him, had the perfect opportunity, and did not take it.* She thought to herself and shook her head angrily. She had learned, in her old age, it does no good to dwell on the past, as it cannot be changed. Nevertheless, it still infuriated her.

John Edwards entered the kitchen. She poured them both some coffee and sat down at the table. She looked at John over her glasses, "Have you heard any word on Louis?"

"No, I have not. It is as if he vanished. The sheriff says he has no clue how he got loose, as he was still unconscious when he was loaded into the back of the wagon. I am not sure whether I believe that or not, but that is what he says. I have known Sheriff Teagan for years and I know he is good people. Faith played with his daughters growing up. I cannot imagine he would have a hand in setting Louis free. He has no way of backtracking. He has no clue when or where Louis got off the wagon. I have searched Ebony's Fall's and the old office behind the bank. He is not at either of those places. I even went to the Saloon and asked the girls if they had seen him. He has not been there either. If I know Louis, and I do, he will rear his head eventually and make his presence known. He always does."

Maw Sally shook her head, "Yes that skunk will come out from hiding. I will be ready when he does. He is so unpredictable; you never know what that fool will do."

"Well, I am going into the study and finish some work and have some brandy. Whatever you are cooking sure smells good."

"I am cooking roast and potatoes," she said.

"That was Faith's favorite." John said.

"Yes, that child sure loved her a good roast. I sure do miss her. I wonder what those two are up to."

"If I know those two, they are up to no good." John laughed jokingly as he walked out of the kitchen.

Maw Sally heard the screen door open and looked up and saw Daisy and Trent enter. Daisy was radiant with her pregnancy belly and smile. Trent helped her to a chair. Maw Sally smiled, "Goodness Chile, how you feeling? You look like you about to pop."

"I am doing good Maw Sally, just getting bigger every day."

Trent smiled, "She gets more beautiful every day to."

"I don't feel beautiful, I feel bloated."

"Well, I love every bloated inch of you." Trent laughed.

"Well pretty soon the baby will be here, and we will have double the love," Daisy smilles.

Maw Sally watched the two smiling. Her mind drifted to Faith and Vayne, and she wondered if they were with child yet. They had promised to visit at least once a month. They were also planning to go back with them to stay at the island sometimes too. She wondered and hoped that they would come home to Edwards Plantation during the stormy season. Hurricanes could be deadly, especially on an island. Trent interrupted her thoughts, "We are fixing to head back to the cabin, we just wanted to stop in and say hi and visit for a spell."

"Not before I send you some of this roast home with you," Maw Sally scolded.

"Well, yes ma'am, that would be mighty nice of you," Trent drawled purposely.

Maw Sally spooned them a big pot of roast and potatoes and added two fried cornbread fritters to the basket and sent them on their way and they bid their goodbyes.

Trent helped Daisy into the wagon. They rode in silence for a while and Trent knew that Daisy had something on her mind. She had been quiet for too long.

"What do you have on your mind? You are too quiet?"

Daisy's face took on a solemn look. "Where do you think Louis is?"

"I honestly don't know. If I know him, he is somewhere plotting," Trent shook his head, "he will show up sooner or later."

"I am terrified for Faith and Vayne, for us to for that matter." Daisy said.

"When he shows his head again, we will get him. You can bet on that." Trent said, as he looked out over the road.

"I am afraid I am not much help with doing anything right now. I just hope I can have the baby and get settled before anything happens."

"You don't worry, I got you covered." Trent knew that he would kill Louis as soon as he saw him. He would just put him out of his misery. He knew that the only way to take care of a rabid dog was to put it down and that is what he intended to do.

They arrived back to the cabin and as they were walking inside, Daisy felt a pain. She knew something was wrong, as she had never had this happen before, but it was excruciating. She stopped and held on to the doorframe as to not fall. Trent ran to her side. "Daisy, what is wrong? It cannot be labor; you are too early for that."

"I don't know what is wrong. I have never had this happen before. Just help me get to the bed so that I can lay down."

Trent picked her up, carried, and sat her down gently on the bed. He was worried, but he would not let her know it. He laid down, gently eased her onto her side, curled in behind her and gently wrapped his arms around her. "We have been riding a lot today and it is too much for you to be jostled around in that wagon. We need to start staying at the cabin and you will rest and keep your feet up. I do not want you cooking or cleaning. We need to take better care of you."

Daisy did not argue. She could not argue that the wagon was not the easiest ride for her these days, especially on the trails with all the bumps and ruts. The sharp pain she felt went away, but it scared her dearly. She knew that Trent was right.

Chapter 4
MONSTROUS REALIZATIONS

Louis Edwards had no clue where he was or where he was going. He barely remembered his name at this point. He could not remember where he was coming from or what had happened. The last thing he remembered is that he was by a stream and chasing Faith. He had no clue why he was chasing her or why they were by Ebony's Falls. He stopped and leaned on a log. *What is going on? Why would Faith be running from me? Better yet, why would I be chasing her?*

Louis rubbed the knot on the back of his head and winced at the pain. It was no longer bleeding out, but the aftereffects were still there. His head felt like someone had clubbed him. His head was still throbbing. He knew that he had to figure this out and understand what had happened. He had no clue where he was or how he had gotten here. He knew he was on a wagon and awoke and had the feeling that he needed to get off the wagon and get away but had no clue why. No matter how hard he tried, he just could not remember anything. He remembered Faith, John, and Maw Sally of course, but it is as if everything else just vanished. He had no clue of his past, present or future. He remembered stopping at a tree, losing his stomach, and seeing the ocean. After that, blackness is all he remembered. *There is no doubt; the pain in the back of my head is the cause of all my confusion.*

He could smell the sea and remembered being lulled to sleep by a steady movement. It was pitch black in the corner where he lay. He saw drums, ropes in piles. He had no clue where he was at right now, but knew by his instinct, that it was better to lay low. He needed to gather his thoughts before he dare to venture out.

He knew he needed to make his way to Edwardstown, he did remember that much about himself. He remembered where home was, but the only problem, he had no clue what awaited him there. He knew from being on the sheriff's wagon that he was evidently in some sort of trouble. He squeezed his eyes shut and realized he could not even remember where he worked at or what he was doing before today. *This is bad. This is unbelievably bad.*

As he drifted off to sleep, flashes went through his mind. Faith was screaming at him; she was running in terror and he was chasing her. He remembered when they were kids and played together by the falls. He saw his mother smiling at him and then gasping as someone put a hand over her mouth to quiet her. He realized it was him putting his hand over his mother's mouth. He tried to cry out and stop, but it was to later, she was gone. Tears ran down his cheeks as he remembered terrible things he had done in his life. *Why did I do this? Why would I willingly kill my mother? Why did I want to hurt Faith?*

Louis opened his eyes when he felt a hand on his arm. He was startled. A Native American woman was in front of him, he heard her words, without her speaking. "I will show you the pain you caused. I will let you feel the pain of others." As she said this, Louis felt anguish. He felt his mother's breath leave her body, he felt Faith's fear and pain. He felt her heartbreak. As all the emotions hit him at once, he was not able to control his sobbing. He called out to his mother and apologized. He called out to Faith and apologized.

Louis was in and out of consciousness with his thoughts and it made him sick to know of the things he had done. *How could I have done these things, and it had not bothered me?* It bothered him now. It made him feel sick on the inside and he felt as if he deserved death. *Sweet Faith. Why did I hurt her so? What kind of a man would do that to another human being, let alone a woman?* He covered his face with his hands as the agony of what he was remembering came rushing back to him. Tears slid down the corners of his eyes and he remembered it all.

He remembered the wrongs he had done and remembered the terror in Faith's eyes as she ran from him. He thought of the sadness in his uncle's eyes as he asked him, "What would your mother think." *I am a monster,* was the last thought he had before he drifted off into a restless fog.

Chapter 5
BLISS AND PROTECTION

Life on the island was peaceful. Faith and Vayne enjoyed working alongside of each other to build a life on the island. Faith looked out over the ocean, caught site of the ship, and wondered if Vayne was restless or genuinely happy being in one place. She knew it must be an adjustment to what he was accustomed to before he met her.

Vayne walked up behind her and wrapped his arms around her, "What are you thinking?"

"I was actually wondering if you were restless and would rather be out on the sea than stuck on an island with me."

Vayne turned her around, "There is no other person I would rather be stuck on an island with. There will be a time when I must go back out to the sea for a bit, but I am content. More content that I have ever been. It is time for me to teach you how to defend yourself in case you need to."

Faith turned toward him, "how will you go about doing that?"

"I am going to start off showing you ways to use your natural weapons. Your natural weapons are your head and feet, among a couple."

"I am not strong though. I am a woman, no match for a man." Faith said.

"It is not about strength. It is about knowing how and where to strike your attacker."

Vayne walked over to her, "Give me your hand. If an attacker is close, you can use your palm to strike the throat. If your attacker leans down toward you, use your thumbs, and go for the eyes."

"I do not think I can do that. I would freeze and not remember any of this." Faith shook her head.

"You are stronger and smarter than you think. We will practice and eventually if will be second nature for you to protect yourself.

"If someone were to come up behind you and put their hand over your mouth, bite. Bite until you taste blood. You must think of your body as a weapon that you can use at any given time. Your body is a weapon that you always have, in any given situation."

Faith was beginning to understand what he meant. She had never really thought about this. "I know what you mean. I used my brain as a weapon when Louis had trapped me in Ebony's Falls, in the cave. I used my brain to outsmart him."

"Now you are talking. That is exactly what I meant." Vayne grinned.

Vayne walked over to Faith and placed a gift of an English Queen Anne cannon barreled flintlock pistol in her hand.

Faith turned it over in her hand stunned, "This is beautiful. I am familiar with rifles and shotguns, but I am afraid, I do not know how to use this."

"I will teach you. You will be a natural, as you are already familiar with guns and shooting. This will make it easier for you to always carry it with you, have access, and be conspicuous, while you carry. We will practice shooting daily until you can hit a bull's eye at any distance."

"I must admit, this excites me. I love shooting and riding. This will help me to be more independent when you are out on the sea."

"That is correct. I will still worry about you, but for naught, because you will be able to take care of anything that you need to." Vayne walked away and set up a bucket on rock, "Now, let us get to practicing. Shoot the dot in the middle."

He walked behind her, she stretched out her arms in front of her, and she rested her right wrist, on top of her left hand between her thumb and other four fingers, to steady her shooting hand. Vayne knew as soon as he saw her do this, that she was indeed a natural.

"Line it up and gently squeeze the trigger." Vayne whispered in her ear.

Faith did not flinch as the barrel exploded and the bucket pinged. Vayne walked to the bucket, turned toward her, and smiled, "Bulls Eye my dear."

Faith smiled to herself. "*I can take care of myself and protect my family. No more scared little girl. I am a wife and will one day be a mother. I will never be afraid again. Not even of a monster.*"

Vayne noticed her smile and saw that she walked a little taller with her shoulders back. He knew that if she was a natural at everything else, he taught her, she would be fine going on some of his trips on The Lady Ebony. She could hold her own. They rarely had any issues with other ships, but if they did, she would be able to deal. He had an idea and some things he needed to buy her that made a little more sense, than the dresses she wore every day. They would be more comfortable too. He would get them soon and gift them to her.

"Well Mrs. Lafitte, I see we do not have to worry about you being able to shoot. You are a natural."

"Well, my father taught me, from the time I was eight, to shoot. I am surprised that I am able to shoot this pistol with ease though," she stated.

"You are going to be simply fine. If I am not around or off the island, you will be able to manage yourself. I feel better about leaving when the time comes."

Faith signed, "I feel better too."

"I gotta get these fences finished so that we can get some livestock here. We need to get this done before the stormy season so we can have things secure. The trees help shield us some, but we have a lot to do to make sure we are ready." Vayne said over his shoulder as he walked away.

"I am going to practice some more. Stew is in the kettle, so it is ready when we are." Faith said as she pulled the gun up and fired off another round at the bucket.

Chapter 6
The Visitor

Vayne was working. The first fence was almost complete. He knew that he had to get the fences set up before the stormy season. He knew that when he went to get the livestock, he might not bring them back until after the season. The area had to be prepared before he brought them home. The sun was hot, as it was nearing August. The bees were buzzing around; he knew that sound meant one thing, that there would be fresh honey for the winter.

He wanted to be as self-sufficient as possible. He had already dug the well and was relieved when he found the freshwater close to the cabin. That meant less trips to the well. He would make a system soon, where he could have it inside the cabin. The outhouse was close to the back door, which would make things easier for Faith, if she were ever to become pregnant. Many things needed to be done. As he was working, he was thinking about Louis. He wondered where he was and what he was doing. He knew that a different storm was brewing inside of him, a storm that consisted of malice. He knew it was eating him up on the inside, and he knew he had to remedy the problem. He shrugged it off. He had other things he needed to think of. Work was always a stress reliever for Vayne even as a child. He remembered working with his mother on the little canoe that she had made. They would go out and fish in the streams and lived off the land. That is what he intended to do here. He wondered if his mother would be proud of the man that he was.

Vayne was walking toward the woods cut some more trees for the fence when he felt a chill to his left. He looked over and he saw a light. The light did not frighten him, but he felt as though it wanted to embrace him. He blinked and standing before him was his beautiful mother. Vayne had not seen her since the last time on the ship when she had warned him of Faith being in danger. Faith walked slowly toward her, he wondered if he had gotten too hot and was seeing apparitions.

"No, my son, I am really here. You are not seeing things.
" He did not hear this voice with his ears but heard it in his heart. He smiled and felt a tear run down his cheek.

"Mother, oh how I miss you. I wish you were still here."

"I am always with you, my son. I am with you every second or every day. We are one and the same. We are attached divinely, and nothing can ever change that. I am very proud of you. Your journey is not over. You will have some trials that you will overcome. You are with your soul mate. She will also have trials. Never give up. Keep the Faith, my son. Always, Keep the Faith."

"Mother, is Faith in danger?" Vayne whispered.

"There are things that you must not know. Some things are not as they appear. You will find a way and figure it out."

"Mother, will we have a child? Please don't go."

"My son, you will be prosperous. Some things come to you, but not as you expect. Keep your heart and mind open. Let any hatred you have go. That hatred only hurts you, not the others."

As she said this, she disappeared as quietly and slowly as she had come.

Vayne stared at the spot she stood for some time. He wiped the tears from his eyes. He knew they were connected. He felt her at times, although he could not see her. It gave him peace that she was always around looking over them. He would keep the Faith.

Chapter 7
Preparing for Sail

After finishing the fences, Vayne knew that he needed to make a trip to the mainland. He needed to get some livestock, seedlings, chickens, and other supplies so that the farm he and Faith were building could be self-sufficient. It would not be long before the stormy season was at full peak, and he may need to take Faith with him and stay on the mainland at Edwards Plantation until it passed. They did not have a storm shelter built yet. He was walking back toward the cabin when Faith stepped outside and handed him a cup of steaming coffee.

"I figured you might enjoy some coffee right about now," she said as she handed him the cup.

"Yes ma'am. You know what I like, Mrs. Lafitte. We are going to have to make a trip to the mainland so that we can get supplies. I want to visit with my grandmother and your father, and I am sure you do to. It has been months since we have seen any of them. I would like to visit with Trent and Daisy. They will have a baby soon. We need to check in and see how they are doing. We should be able to get to the mainland in two says, providing we do not run into any storms." Vayne sipped his coffee.

"I agree. I cannot wait to see everyone. I am excited to see Daisy. I bet her belly has grown immensely since we saw them last."

Vayne grinned, "Yes I bet it has. I bet Trent loves every second of it."

"When do you want to leave and go to the mainland," Faith asked.

"We will leave in a few days. I need to get the men ready and make sure we get the barrels loaded and everything ready for livestock when we bring them back."

Vayne made his way down to the ship to search out Paddy. He found him sitting on the desk sipping on his ale while he was fishing.

"Hey Paddy. Anything biting?"

"Aye, just little turd tappers, not worth keeping. I threw them back." Paddy grinned is snaggle toothed grin as she answered Vayne. Vayne had to hold back a chuckle, as he could tell that Paddy had been sipping quite a while on the ale, as his words slurred, and his Scottish accent was even thicker.

"Well, we have got to ready the ship to make a trip to the mainland. Gather the men and have them get things ready. We are bringing back livestock from the mainland and some fowl. So, make sure that we have what we need for them. I will check the rigging and such, while you all get below ready. We will leave in two days' time."

"Aye. I will get everyone together and get it started. Now that we have you Double Clews if Miss Faith accompanying us?"

"You are a good man Paddy, but she will not be going with us this time." Vayne slapped him on the back and laughed as he walked away.

Paddy made is way below deck to assess the storage area to see what work needed completing, to get it ready for the cargo and animals that they needed to bring back. They had already gotten things in order a while back, but he knew that here were other tasks that needed to be completed. He entered the cargo holding and stared to move barrels toward the walls to store seedlings, grains and of course ale. His favorite. He was busying working when he pulled back a barrel and noticed a makeshift bed. Puzzled her scratched his head, walked closer, and noticed that a half empty can with water sat there. He knew this was out of place, as the men slept in the hammocks on the other side. Paddy scratched his head. *What is this doing here? Did one of the men move here for privacy? This was unusual, as the men usually congregated and talked in the evenings when the sun went down. This was very odd indeed.*

Paddy shook his head and took note and went about his business. He finished the barrels and started to place up the pens for the livestock. The crates for the hens would be in the corner in the back. They would be relaxed there, so eggs should be plentiful. He covered the floors of the pens with burlap so that the livestock could do their business and cleanup easier when they got back to the island. He moved the troughs for water along with the feeders near the outside of the pens so that the animals could easily stay hydrated. He knew that it would be hot, and they would need plenty of nourishment to be in good health during the trip. He checked the ducts and opened the dorade box, to keep fresh air flowing below.

The other men came below to help assemble the last remaining pens. Each took about their task with ease. Paddy asked the men if any of them had a makeshift bed in the back and each man shook his head no. Paddy did not know what to make of what he found, but just let it go. He went on deck to make sure that the dory was secure. *Better safe than sorry*, he thought.

Chapter 8
Snake Ashore

Louis awoke and noticed that his headache was gone and eased to stand up. All the men on the ship were asleep. He was not surprised, as they had been drinking and talking for hours. He made his way slowly to the door and stopped when it creaked to see if any of the men stirred awake. None did. He eased up the stairs and made his way to the deck. He did not want to be discovered on this ship. He had been waiting for the right opportunity and this was it. He eased down the ladder and felt the water enter his boots as he eased down. He made his way to the short. It was pitch black and no one else nearby.

He followed the boot prints in the sand to the edge of the woods. He could see the trail that was leading into the woods. He did not know where the trail lead to, but he did know that he had to get off the shore before he saw seen. He entered the woods and wished immediately that he had a torch. He stumbled and cursed to himself.

As he made his way down the trail, it opened and he saw the soft glow of candles coming from the windows in a cabin. He knew he could not go there, but he quietly made his way so that he could get a closer look. As he drew nearer, he saw Faith and Vayne in an embrace in front of the window. *Where am I? That is Faith and a man. He looks familiar but I do not know why. Why is she here instead of at the plantation? Where is here?*

Louis dashed to the side of the house and made his way towards the woods again, to stay out of sight. As he walked through the woods, his mind was racing. He was trying to put the pieces together in his mind. As he saw the woods open, he saw the lighthouse. He made a run for it and made his way inside. *I can take shelter here, at least for the night. I will have to get a game plan and figure out what to do.*

Louis made his way to the spiral staircase and went to the top floor. He could see that construction was going on and figured this was the safest place right now, as it was not in the best shape there. As he crawled over the wooden boards on the floor, he saw a shadow out of the corner of his eye. When he turned to look, nothing was there. He felt the hairs on his arms bristle. He shook his head. *Must be the knot on my head again making me delirious.* He took off his jacket, rolled it up, used it as a pillow, and let sleep overtake him.

Louis dreamt of animals chasing him on the island. A black panther was circling him. He could feel her hot breath on his neck as he ran. As he glanced back, the black panther, became a black bear, he could hear the growling as it neared him. Tossing and turning throughout the night, he dreamt of a beautiful, Native American woman. She was coming toward him. He knew she was trying to get him to follow her. He knew that if he followed her, he would never come back. She had a sadness in her eyes. She knew all the evil that he had done in his life. He was ashamed and put his head down. He ached to follow her but was afraid. The last thing he saw, before she disappeared, is a glimpse of Faith and the man he had saw earlier in front of him with a look of pure anger.

Chapter 9
Trip To the Mainland

The men were busy readying the ship. Vayne was checking the cabin and making sure things were in order. This was the first time he was leaving Faith here alone on the island do a run to the mainland for supplies. He had no doubt she could handle herself, but it still made him nervous to leave her.

"You have the gun loaded and put away with easy access?" Vayne asked.

"Yes. I have it beside my bad tucked away. Stop worrying. I will be fine."

"I don't have a doubt you will be fine. I just wanted to double check."

"We will be gone a week at the most. I am leaving two of the men behind. I am taking Paddy, but Slade and Benoit will stay here to keep an eye on things." Vayne said as he hoisted his pack and threw it over his shoulder. "They have strict orders to make sure you are safe and that they are within ear shot if you need them. They have set up homestead just through the woods. Once we get back, I am going to help all my men set up their own parcel so that they can be comfortable, when we are not sailing."

"You just get our supplies and whatever else you are bringing back. I am perfectly fine here. Next time I can go with you."

"Yes, I want you to go with me. If I were not trying to get all the livestock to bring back, I would take you this time. It is going to be some rough sailing, if we run into severe weather, especially this time of year. We are nearing hurricane season and we are trying to get back in time to get things settled here and then we both will head back to Edwards Plantation to stay safe."

Faith leaned up on her tiptoes and gave him a kiss. I will be waiting on you when you get back. With that, Vayne gave her one last kiss on top of the head, walked out the door, and shut it behind him.

Vayne walked through the woods and towards Slade and Benoit's cabins. He wanted to check in with them before he headed to the ship.

"I am heading out now," he said to Benoit as he approached him.

"Things will be fine boss. Slade and I can manage things while you are gone. The missus will be fine." Benoit was a short, stocky man. Reddish hair and a short beard covered his face. He and Vayne had been friends for years. Vayne knew he could trust him.

"Where is Slade?" Vayne asked.

"He is probably headed back from the ship about now."

"I will head to the ship; I will probably meet him on the path." Vayne turned and headed down the path toward the ship. As he was about the get to the end of the trail, he saw Slade. Slade was a tall brut. Wide shoulders, jet-black hair, muscles from head to toe with a black beard that looked like a raven perched on his face.

"Slade, I was hoping to run into you. I am fixing to leave for the mainland. I wanted to check in with you to make sure you have everything in order and to remind you to keep an eye on Faith, while I was gone."

"Yes. I got everything we should need. If a storm were to come, I will go and get Miss Faith and make sure she is safe and taken care of."

"Good that is what I like to hear. We have a storm cellar under the cabin, but it is not finished yet. I dug it out myself but have not had time to stone the walls yet and I do not think it would be safe to get into." Vayne said looking off.

Slade smiled, "I found a cave in the woods. It is high altitude and would be safe, if we needed to go somewhere in a storm."

"How far it is away from our cabin and yours?"

"Not far, it is up the hill. It is facing away from the sea, so if a storm comes the entrance is away from where the winds will be coming from."

"Nice job Slade. You need to show it to me when I get back. We can make that a storm shelter. Sounds like the perfect spot."

"Aye sir. Will do." With this, Slade slapped Vayne on the back and started into the woods.

As Vayne was boarding the sip, he saw Paddy. He smiled to himself. He knew that if something happened, and he was not able to steer this ship, that Paddy could take over and manage it himself.

"Are we ready sale Paddy?"

"Aye. We are ready as we ever will be."

With this, they hoisted the sales, and the ship started for the mainland. The skies were clear, but Vayne knew that could change at any time. He set sail for the mainland on the coastline. He felt the familiar wind in his face and the smell of the sea and smiled to himself. *I have sorely missed you.*

Chapter 10
Stormy at Home and at Sea

As Vayne made his way out into open seas, it felt good smelling the salt air and feeling the breeze on his face. It was not lost on him that there was an eerie feeling in the air. He knew that a storm somewhere, he could smell it. He learned a long time ago, that he had a sense when tides were turning and knew when to pay attention. The ship caught some good wind in its sails and was moving at a steady pace. That sudden gust got his attention.

"Paddy, make sure that everything is tied down and secure. I sense a storm coming and we don't want to be caught off guard."

"Aye, I already handled that. I got the senses in me bones myself." Paddy replied.

"I should have known you were already on top of it old friend."

Vayne focused on getting the ship as close to the mainland before the storm caught up to them. His thoughts went to the island. He regretted leaving now. He knew Faith could take care of herself, but that did not stop him from worrying. He knew that Benoit and Slade would help her, if the need arose, but it did not mean he felt good about it. He knew that they would not make landfall before nightfall, as it was a two-day journey at least, depending on how high the winds got in his sails.

It was midnight, when the first raindrops started to fall. It started slowly, then the thunder started, and all hell broke loose. The rain was coming in sheets and Vayne could not tell which way was forward. The ship tossed and turned, like a cork on the end of a rod. Up and down the ship tossed and Vayne did all he could just to hold on to the wheel.

Waves splashed onto the deck and the men eventually tied themselves to the sides, to stay aboard. Vayne knew that this was the worst storm he had encountered in years. He also knew that rain was not the only thing that storms could throw at you. He had seen squalls that would sink a ship in a matter of seconds. He was hoping that he and his men did not have to encounter this. The moon was nowhere in sight, and it was pitch black out. Between the rain and clouds, it was easy to become lost in these open waters. Vayne was very much aware of this.

Faith noticed the dark clouds on the horizon, and she fetched waster from the well. She knew that she needed to get things ready, as she could tell that a storm was coming. As she drew water from the well, she made a list of things that she needed to get ready. She knew that she would draw the shutters closed and make sure she had plenty of water and firewood inside, as she did not know how long the storm would last. She was not scared of storms, but she also respected what they could do.

She made her way inside and poured the water into the barrel. She knew that she would need to make several more trips to make sure she had enough. After several trips, the barrel was full. Now it was time to gather the firewood. She needed to bring it inside, so that it would stay dry. After she gathered the firewood, and stacked it neatly by the fireplace, she set about moving anything that could cause damage into the storm shelter they had not yet completed. At least in there, it would not blow around and cause damage outside. She was proud of herself as she looked around and realized she was ready to settle in. She had already filled the pantry with cans of vegetables and jerky for the winter. Now it was time to sit and wait. She also had her needlepoint ready and books to pass the time. She closed and locked the shutters. Brought the latch down across the front door and back door, stoked the fire and sat down in her rocking chair by the fireplace. It was time to settle in for the duration of this storm.

Louis saw the clouds rolling from the top of the lighthouse. He swallowed hard, as he had no clue what he was going to do. He could not go to the cabin and seek shelter from Faith. She would kill him on sight. *Who could blame her?* He winced. He saw the man leave the island with the ship. He was surprised that he left Faith to fend for herself. Of course, a ship is no place for a woman. *Only men could oversee that task*, he thought. He was jolted out of thoughts with a bright bolt of lightning and winced as he began to make his way to the bottom floor of the lighthouse. *I have no food, water, or way to build a fire. This is going to be a long, hard night.* His stomach growled at him as he crawled into the far back corner and prepared to hunker down.

Maw Sally was washing dishes as she looked at the window and noticed clouds in the distance. As John Edwards walked into the kitchen, Maw Sally said over her shoulder, "There is quite a storm a brewing. We best start getting things in order. I am afraid we are in for a bad one."

"I noticed that when I was feeding the horses. Looks like some mean clouds headed our way."

"We are in for more than clouds. The devil himself fixing to send the storm hounds our way. We best get to work. We need to batten down the hatches because this is going to be bad."

Maw Sally set about her yearly routine of readying the plantation for the storms. "I will go and gather the eggs, potatoes and whatever else is ready. Then we can start pouring up water."

John nodded to her, "Yes, I will start closing the shutters when it gets time, right now we can open some windows and enjoy the breeze. I will make sure to round up all the livestock and get them settled in with plenty of grain and water. We need to move the wagons to the barn also and make sure we have plenty of kerosene for the lanterns and lamps."

"I will go ahead and get us some stew made up in the kettle and some corn fritters and biscuits. I need to keep me busy. This season makes me nervous." Maw Sally said as she started toward the back screen door.

Trent headed home from town and felt the wind when it picked up. He knew that he needed to get home, there was a storm coming and he did not want Daisy there by herself, any longer than she had to be. He had loaded the wagon down with supplies so that they would have anything that they needed. This time of the year was trying living right on the coastline, but the rest of the year made up for it. He had tried to get Daisy to go and stay at the doc's house, in case something arose with the baby, but she refused. *Stubborn woman,* he thought. As he entered the cabin, Daisy was busying herself with tidying up. He knew that she was nervous about the storm coming. He also knew that she was not far from the baby making an entrance. It could happen any day now. They had the crib and supplies on hand. He just hoped that they would not have to use them, before this storm blows over.

"Daisy, are you sure you don't want to go and stay at Edwards Plantation? We were asked to come there and stay for the storm."

"No, I would rather be there in our home. I do not like the thought of leaving everything. What if we cannot get back into the cabin and something happens?"

Trent knew he was going against his better judgement by staying, but he did not want Daisy to uneasy or stressed, "Okay, it is your call. We will stay."

Ms. Alma was getting the bookstore ready for the storm. She dreaded this time of year. She had a list of tasks that she knew she had to be done to make sure the damage was minimal, especially to all her precious books. She wished Vayne were here to help her; *this is a lot of work for an old woman.* She pulled the shelves to the middle of the room. *I am glad I have these on wheels now.* She pulled the storm shutters to on the front of the store and turned the closed sign around as she went out the door and headed to Edwards Plantation. She planned to ride out the storm at the Plantation with Mr. Edwards and Maw Sally. She did not want to be alone, and at the request for John Edwards, had become a resident at the plantation. *According to John, we all are family now and family sticks together.* She really enjoyed being around family and life. She was getting lonely living all by herself. She missed Vayne and Faith and being at the plantation helped her to feel that void. She did consider them her only family now. She intended to spend the rest of her life relishing in the fact that she now had a family, and a good one at that.

Chapter 10
Destruction

Vayne did not fear much, but Mother Nature could be fickle. It was all he could do to hold tight and keep the ship on course. He was sure which direction they were in now. He thinks he kept the ship headed in the right direction, but until this storm blew over, he was not certain. The men were tired and drenched. Paddy was struggling. Vayne could see it. *Paddy was not getting any younger and Vayne often worried how much longer he could keep on these voyages.* Paddy had been with Vayne since he acquired his first ship. Paddy was the one constant in his life until he met Faith. A father figure of sorts, he had sought Patty's counsel on more than one occasion.

The sound snapped Vayne out of his thoughts. He heard the familiar pop of the line as the mast swung forward in a jerking motion. The wind flung it like a weapon. As Vayne turned to yell a warning, it was too late, the broken mast struck Paddy in the back of the head and as his eyes glazed over, Vayne knew he was gone. He saw life leave his body and his eyes at the same time. The screaming Vayne heard was his, although he did not realize it. "Paddy! Paddy!" The men pulled Vayne off Paddy, "He is gone sir. He is gone" Vayne, who never showed emotion in front of his men, had no control over himself in this moment.

The men backed away and let him through. "Sir, we got this, go below for a bit."

"I am fine." Vayne hoisted Paddy up and took him below. As he got below, he laid Paddy on his bed. He knew that he had to cover him and get him below. Vayne was not ready to let go of him yet. Tears flowed freely in the privacy of his quarters. It was rare that Vayne had ever cried. Three times in his life. Once when his mother left, twice, when Faith was attacked and now, Paddy, the first father figure he ever knew is gone. In his grief, Vayne lost track of time. He did not know how long he sat there with his head down and dealing with such a huge loss. His heart ached, he felt as though it would stop beating. *I should have had all the men go below. I should not have had Paddy on deck. Who am I kidding? I could not have stopped him if I tried too. He loved this life.*

It was in that moment that he realized just how fast life can change. He knew, that at any moment, life could be taken from you and change your world forever. He also realized that time was of the essence. He needed to live every moment as if it is your last.

Vayne wrapped Paddy in a blanket and took him below deck. This would have to do until they could get through this storm. Paddy would be buried at sea. That is what he would have wanted.

Farewell Poem to Paddy

Paddy did it all, First Mate, Quartermaster, Sailing Master, from Gunner to Cook.
A Powder Monkey somedays and a Boatswain on others could do it all and was never shook.
A wee man in stature, but a giant of heart,
Paddy did it all, from the very start.
He was not only my friend, but also family in the heart.
He will be missed. He was loved by all.
We were his family, as he had none that I recall.
A burial at sea is what he will get,
It is what he wanted, as he always said.
Farewell to Paddy, ride on the waves.
Until we see you again, your spirit remains.
Vayne Lafitte,
Captain: The Lady Ebony
Logged: Oct 1, 1840, The day we lost Paddy.

Chapter 11
Burial At Sea

As Vayne ascended from below, the mood was solemn and quiet on deck. Vayne did not know how long he had been below. It must have been hours, as it was now light out. His chest was still tight, but the emotions of losing his best mate, but he knew that he had to be stoic. He noticed the weariness of his men. He knew that this was a hard blow to them also. They were a sea family. Most of his men had no real family to speak of, except their fellow crewmembers. This was the first loss in many a year. This was the biggest loss, any of them had ever experienced. The men busied themselves, but Vayne knew they were hurting. Hell, he was hurting deep within his soul. There would never be another Paddy.

Vayne knew that they had to get the ship back in order and then prepare for their first burial at sea. He had a lot to do and think about. Vayne stepped up and cleared his throat.

"Men, I know that this is a tough time. Even for us hard legs. However, we must get The Lady Ebony back in working order. The storms have cleared now, so we will anchor here and get to work. I know this had been a long hard night and I know you are tired. We will push forward, as we always do. We will come together as the crew, that we are, and get this turned around. Once we get things back in order and place, we will prepare to give Paddy the burial that he deserves."

As the men stood there watching Vayne, he heard "Aye" slowing roll across the men's tongues. He knew that this was a tribute to their mate. Vayne smiled, "Aye, aye, for Paddy." As the crewmembers started to chant, Vayne felt a tear slide down his cheek, "Aye, aye for Paddy."

The minutes turned into hours, but Vayne and the men worked and got the ship back in order and sails repaired. As the work ended, Vayne went below to prepare Paddy for burial. He knew he had to get the shroud finished and weighted to sew Paddy into it. Vayne winced at the thought of it, but knew it was the proper thing to do. He went below and started about his work. Vayne took his time as to honor his friend as he set about preparing him for burial. He went back on deck and advised the men to ready the cannons; there would be three powerful shots from the cannons, in respect to his duty. The flags lowered to half mask.

Vayne slowly carried Paddy up onto top deck. As the men lined up, on each side, each placed a hand on the shroud as Vayne passed through the middle. Quietly Vayne walked toward the side of the ship and the plank lowered. Slowly he placed Paddy onto the ramp, feet facing down and slowly lowered him to the sea. As the body floated and then started to sink, the cannons fired in unison, once, twice then three times. Vayne felt as though he could not breathe in that very moment and knew that a tiny piece of his heart was at the bottom of the sea with his dear friend and mentor.

Chapter 12
Island of Survival

Faith heard the rain as it started. The wind was picking up, and she looked at the window, she could see the dark clouds as they started to roll in. She had an eerie feeling. She did not know why she was feeling this way. She has never been afraid of storms. She secretly loved them. She loved the sound of the rain, and it relaxed her. She loves watching the lightning. It could not contain, kind of like her. She loved the beauty of it. Lightning has a mind of its own and she liked that. It was not lost on her, the danger of it. That was part of the excitement.

She knew that she was ready for the storm. She had plenty of water; she closed the shutters and locked them up. She had a stockpile of food and wood for cooking. She even had books to keep her busy and plenty of kerosene and candles. Vayne had made sure she had all the essentials.

I hope Vayne and the crew are okay, she thought.

She had no doubt that Vayne could handle himself, but Mother Nature could be a beast, when she chose to act up. Shivers ran up her spine as she thought about him out on the sea in this storm.

Please come back to me safe.

Faith awoke to the sound of thunder and rain. She could tell, by the sound, the storm was getting close, as it was raging outside. Rain pelted on the roof, and she knew better than to open the door and peek out, as she may not be able to get it shut again. It was dark as she made her way to the kitchen to light a lantern to put on a kettle of coffee. She struck the match and lit the lantern. She loved the smell of a burning match. It reminded her of when she was little. Maw Sally would always light the lanterns and it took her mind back to home. She missed everyone so much. She hoped that they would fair okay in this storm. She hoped they all were prepared. Her mind drifted to the ship and her husband.

Faith did not like being alone. She would be glad when she could hear the pitter patter of little feet echoing through the cabin. She pushed that thought out of her mind. She set about the task of cooking a couple of eggs and a piece of ham. If she could not do anything else, she could cook and eat. She was growing restless. The coffee was a welcome distraction, as the bitter taste hit her tongue. She stoked the fireplace, added a piece of wood, sat on the couch, and decided to read. An enjoyable book was always a welcome distraction.

Faith was startled awake from a crash. She bolted upright on the couch and the book tumbled to the floor. She could hear the wind howling outside. She did not know what the crash was, but it was loud. She stood up from the couch and ran to the window. It was as if a black blanket had covered the window. She could see a glimmer of the front porch, when the lightning flashed, however, once the lightning stopped, she saw nothing but blackness.

She knew that this was just the beginning, and it made her nervous. She could feel the electricity in the air, and it made the hair on her arms stand. It was one thing for a storm to come during the day, but an entirely different story when it happened at night. It seemed scarier. Faith turned at the sound of water. She picked up the lantern and saw that something had hit the window over the kitchen sink. As she got closer, she saw it was a limb.

She pulled the limb inside and had absolutely no clue how what to cover this window with. She made her way to the front door and took a deep breath as she reached to open it. She decided not to try to open the door, for fear of the wind and being able to get it closed back. She turned and remembered upstairs she has saw tack cloth and nails. As she made her way to the desk upstairs, she got the nails, but knew the minute she picked up the cloth, that is would not work. It would be too thin. As she made her way back downstairs, she saw the animal skin rug and decided it would work. She picked it up and made her way back to the window. As she was holding the rug in one hand and the nail in the other, she braced herself for loud thunder as the lightning lit up the outside. She caught a glimmer of something, or someone, and it startled her. She blinked, and it was gone. She did not have time to worry about this; she had to get this window covered.

She set about the task of handing the rug and tacking it snugly around the window. As she finished this tasked, she was proud of herself, as the skin was thick enough to keep out the rain and wind. Faith knew enough to be able to gauge how far the lightning was by counting in between the time the skies lit up to when she heard the sound. The storm had arrived, but she feared the worst was yet to come.

Faith heard a tap at the door. It made her nervous as she walked toward it. As she cracked the door, she saw a huge man there.

"Ma'am, my name is Slade. I am a friend of your husbands."

"Yes, of course, come in. Vayne told me that you were here. How are you faring with this storm?"

"We are okay; I wanted to check in on you. We are in for a quite a night. This is only the beginning." Slade said as he took off his rain-soaked hat.

Faith took his hat and hung it by the door. "Come in, it is nice to know someone is here. Sit down and I will get you coffee" Faith walked to the kitchen and poured him a cup. As she walked back to the couch, she handed him the cup, "How do you think Vayne and the crew are managing this storm?"

"They are doing well. This is not the first storm they have encountered. Vayne is a great captain and has a good crew. They are in open seas letting the wind do all the work." He smiled and sipped the coffee. He knew she was worried. He was a little worried himself but would not let Faith know. He knew it would do her no good. They needed to focus on handling things here. Vayne could take care of himself.

"I sure hope you are right. I cannot imagine being out on the seas with all this wind and rain." Faith blinked and shook her head.

Slade looked over at the window over the sink and smiled, "I see you handled the window situation pretty well." He nodded toward the sink.

"Yes, gave me a fright when the limb hit it. That is all I could think to do." She laughed.

"Well, I would have done the same." Slade winked. "I think I will stay close, just in case anything else happens."

Faith sighed, "As much as I hate to admit it, I would like for you to stay close. I would enjoy the company honestly."

"Well, it is settled. Benoit is around here somewhere. Have you met him yet?"

"No, I have not met him, but Vayne did tell me he was here also."

"Yes, I am expecting he will make his way here soon to check on you. I think its best we all stay together. With this storm and all, be wise. If that is okay with you. I mean, I know some women worry about being around two big brutes and worry what others might think. You know we on an island and all, we would not want the seagulls to talk."

Faith threw her head back and laughed, "Oh I have never really cared what others think, especially sea gulls. If you are friends of my husbands and he trusted you enough to leave you here with me, then I am okay with it to."

Slade laughed and knew in that moment, why his friend loved this woman.

"Well, it is settled then. We will all ride this storm out together." Slade stood up and walked toward the door, "Let me find Benoit and get him rounded up. We will be back here later. We need to get things finished and secured."

"See you in a bit," Faith said.

Chapter 13
Two Brutes

Slade walked down the steps toward the wood line. He looked out over the ocean, and he knew that this storm was going to get bad. He just prayed no tornadoes appeared. This was a beautiful island, but during this season, it could get very ugly. The rain was coming down hard when he saw Benoit. "We need to get finished and go back to the main cabin. We are going to hunker down with Ms. Faith." Slade said as he walked up.

"She okay with that?" Benoit asked.

"Yep. We discussed it and it would be better for all of us to stick close and together."

"Alright. I got everything boarded up. You got your stuff taken care of?"

Slade thought for a minute, "I have to go check the light house and then I will be done."

"C'mon, I will go help you and then we get back to the cabin." Benoit said over his shoulder as he turned and started walking.

The two men made their way toward the lighthouse. They had stashed planks there earlier. They needed to board up as many windows as they could, to keep damage to a minimum. As the two men made their way to the lighthouse, they both saw the figure and vague light at the same time and stopped.

Slade leaned over and whispered, "Is that a candlelight?"

"Appears to be, but who? Is Ms. Faith at the cabin?" Benoit trying to be quiet.

"She was the last time I checked, and I don't see any reason she would be out in this weather."

The men started to ease their way toward the light, as they got closer, the light disappeared, and they both stopped. They were confused. It was there and then it was gone.

"Who the hell was that?" Benoit asked.

"We need to find out. No one else should be here right now." Slade said as he picked up his pace.

They both got the lighthouse, opened the door.

Slade looking around, "Who is in here? You need to come out so we can see you."

Benoit heard a noise to his right, as the wood splintered across his head, "Son of a" He did not finish his sentence.

The dark figure lurched passed them and was gone into the night. Slade helped Benoit up.

"You Hurt?" Slade said helping him to his feet.

"Just my pride. Whatever that was will be hurting when I am finished with it."

Both men knew there was no use in chasing whoever that was. In this darkness and rain, they had no clue which way they went. They knew that they needed to get back to the cabin with Faith, sooner than later.

As they finished the lighthouse and made it back toward the cabin, both men pondered whom that could have been earlier. Where did the person go and did, they mean harm? Whoever it was, will have a tough time out in the weather.

Both men reached the porch at the same time. Faith opened the door as she heard them.

"You both come in, I have some stew for you and some coffee," Faith said.

She stepped aside and sat them down at the table. The two men did not mention the figure they saw before; they did not want to worry her. They glanced at each other and did not have to speak, both knew.

"Ms. Faith, it is going to be a long night. You might want to get rest if you can." Slade said.

"Call me Faith. Both of you." She smiled.

"Yes maam."

"I will get rest later. I dozed off earlier while reading. I am not tired. Besides, we all need to keep an eye on things."

The two men knew there was no point in arguing with a woman. They would not win. Both men grinned.

Benoit sat forward, "Well we got the lighthouse taken care of and boarded up."

Slade joined in, "We got everything else around here taken care of. Now all we must do is wait it out and fix any damage as it happens. I am praying that does not happen."

"Me to," Faith smiled.

"You boys eat up. I have wood inside to keep it dry. I have water stored and we are good on other supplies. I just hope Vayne and the crew are well."

Both men glanced at each other. They were hoping Vayne and crew were safe also. They were aware of how bad it could get out on the seas, especially in a storm.

Chapter 14
The Hole

Louis was not sure if he was seeing shadows from the storm or someone approaching the lighthouse. He picked up the piece of wood that he tripped over earlier. As the shapes got closer, he could tell it was two men. Two big men. His heart was racing as he braced himself. As they entered the lighthouse, he swung. He felt contact made with one and from the cursing; he knew he had hit one of them. He sprinted from the door and had no clue which way he was running. As he got further away, he did not know if they were chasing him. He felt as if he was blind as he made his way. He had no direction, just ran as fast as his feet would carry him. His mind was racing.

I hate this! I wish I were back home on Edwards Plantation. I am destined for disaster. I just want to go home. I want this all to be a dream. How did I turn into this person? Did it start as a kid? Am I a walking demon?

Confused thoughts raced through his mind. He was unsure of what he was running from. He did not even know why he had done the things that he did. He felt like an animal. An animal that did not even know why he existed. He was cold, wet, and hungry. Oh, he was so hungry. He thought he was dreaming as he saw a flicker of light in the distance. He had no clue how far he had run, but he had hope when he saw the flicker from the cabin. He slowed to a pace.

He was sure if they were chasing him. Surely, if they were, they would have caught up to him by now. As he crept to the window by the porch, he caught a glimpse of Faith through the window. He knew he could not enter the cabin. Not right now. He knew her reaction would not be good. After what he had done to her, who would blame her. He knew that there was no way he could shelter here. It was pitch black and he could barely see anything, except shadows.

He noticed a lantern on the porch and remembered he had the friction lights in his pocket. He eased the lantern from the porch and made his way around the house. He tripped and noticed a hold. He carefully balanced the lantern in his hand, got on his knees, and crawled toward the hole.

As he crawled inside, it opened. As he got into the hold, under the house, he lit the lantern. As he looked around, he saw the tools leaned up against the dirt walls. Someone had dug this out and he could only guess it was going to be a cellar or storm shelter of sorts. *I will stay here and keep out of sight.* He heard his stomach rumble and reminded him he had not had solid food in days. He heard the thunder and saw the lightning through the hole outside. He was glad he found somewhere, no matter how dirty, to stay dry.

Will I ever get back home? What will happen when if I do get back home? I do not know what to do. God help me. How fitting that I am laying in a hole. I surely have dug myself a hole, and I am sure that I will be buried in it.

He leaned back on the dirt wall and closed his eyes, praying that this was all just a bad dream.

Chapter 15
Porch Talk and a Message

Alma and Maw Sally sat on the porch watching the clouds roll in. "I wonder how Daisy is doing." Ms. Alma said.

"Oh I am sure she feels like she is about to pop. That baby should be arriving anytime now." Maw sally said, as she threw the last of the beans she was shelling into her pot.

"It sure will be nice to have a new baby around." Alma shifted in the rocking chair.

Maw Sally smiled, "Yes. It will be nice to spoil a baby. It has been many years since we had a little one around here."

Alma smile, "I remember when Vayne was just a wee boy. He was very stubborn, but it has served him well."

"Faith was as stubborn as a mule. Still is." Maw Sally threw back her head and laughed.

"Yes she is. Gets it from her mother. Her mother was a very independent woman, in her day." Edward said as he walked onto the porch with lemonade for both women. He handed both women a glass and took the tray back into the house.

"He is right you know. Mrs. Edwards was a beautiful strong woman and Faith reminds me of her so much. She was a force to be reckoned with." Maw Sally was lost in memories as she glanced over at Ms. Alma. "What is wrong Ms. Alma?" She noticed Ms. Alma was sitting up staring into the distance.

"Look at them clouds," she pointed into the distance. "This storm is going to be a bad one. I hate storms."

Maw Sally saw the dark clouds. "Sometimes it takes a storm to purge the land."

Ms. Alma sat back, "This looks like it will purge more than the land."

Maw Sally started to hum and sing the rain dance song of her people, "Come again, come again, come good rain. Fall upon the mountains and on the plain. Come again, come again, come good rain. Water for the river and for the grain."

She remembered this song since she was a small child. It made her think of Ebony, her sweet daughter. Tears slid down her cheeks as she reminisced, and memories of her daughter came flooding back. She could almost reach out and touch her daughters face, as she closed her eyes and saw her. *Oh, my sweet Ebony. I miss you so. If you could see your son now. See the man he has become.*

"I see him, Agitsi. I am with you both." Maw Sally smiled as she heard her daughter's voice. She knew she was not dreaming, as she felt the feather light kiss on her cheek. She remembered that Agitsi means mother. It had been many moons since she heard her native language. As Maw Sally opened her eyes, she saw a butterfly, and it landed on her hand. She smiled, as she knew this was a good omen, meaning transformation and balance was coming. Something that she needed in this time. Ebony was letting her know that all was well. This relieved Maw Sally and peace settle over her.

"Ms. Alma, everything is going to be okay. There will be a rainbow after this storm."

Ms. Alma smiled, "I hope you are right. I really do."

Chapter 16
The Dream

Vayne bid his men good night and made his way below. He was wet and bone tired. He knew that he had to rest. He has been up for hours with no rest. He had helped The Lady Ebony battle the storms. It was brutal. *The old girl held up.* Vayne smiled to himself. He knew his men could handle it, while he got some shuteye.

As Vayne drifted off to sleep, he felt the familiar presence of his mother. He did not need to open his eyes to see her. She was with him always. She was in a field covered in white flowers. She was holding the hand of a warrior. Vayne felt as if he was following them. He smiled as he saw how tender this warrior was with his mother. The warrior was tall, lean, and muscular. Long dark hair with a headdress. He knew he was a chief. The chief reached down, touched Ebony's face, bent down, and kissed her lightly. Then he reached down and touched her belly. Vayne's took in a breath. He did not understand what he was seeing.

The scene changed. He was standing watching a village. He was watching his native people, which included women and children, slaughtered, raped, and murdered. He saw the chief in the distance on his white stallion riding in. His face was painted. He was indeed a warrior. He killed as he rode. Vayne was in awe of the swiftness he was able to take aim and hit his mark. Vayne saw his mother, riding with the chief. She was almost majestic as she took her aim and fought. She was a warrioress. She rode with the grace and her head up with pride. Her long black hair flew behind her and reminded him of a raven. She was fast and was able to keep up with the chief. They rode as if they were one. Vayne knew that this was not their first time in battle together.

As Vayne watched, in his mind's eye, the scene changed again. This time, his mother was in the village alone and he saw men ride in, that did not belong. He saw the man, he knew him. This was Al. The man that claimed to be his father. The man he killed. Vayne watched in horror as they attacked Ebony. He turned his head, as he knew what was going to happen. His pregnant mother. The warrioress. Vayne knew instantly why Ebony was showing him these images. He knew exactly who he was. He was the son of a Chief and Princess. The son of a warrior and a warrioress. With the realization, his mother appeared in front of him and smile.

"My son, you see. You were no bastard. I was with child, prior. Your father was a brave warrior. His blood runs through your veins. You are his son. Stand proud my son. Stand proud and know that you had two parents that loved you. You are not a product of violence. You are a product of the tenderness of your father. The love we have for each other. We are always with you." Ebony spoke without moving her lips.

Tears streamed down Vayne's face, at the realization that he was not a product of a rape. He was not the son conceived through a gruesome act. He was a product of love. Vayne felt the weight lifted from his shoulders. A weight he did not realize he was carrying, until this very moment. Vayne wanted to stay with his mother, but he knew it was time for her to go. She touched his face, "I will see you again. There is more for you to learn. You deserve to know where you came from and how you got to where you remember. I can give you that gift. I love you."

When Vayne awoke, he saw light streaming into his cabin. It had been hours since he came below. It only seemed like a moment. His father was not a monster. The monster he killed had no kindship to him. As he rose to get dressed, he felt as if he could fly. The weight he had been carrying was gone.

Chapter 17
Cabin Fever

Trent was busying planking up the windows and getting the cabin in order to ride out the storm. He dreaded staying here, but what Daisy wants, Daisy gets. Her being with child, Trent knew this was not a clever idea. They should be either at the doc's or at Edwards Plantation. Against his better judgement, he agreed.

"You about finished with everything?" Daisy asked as she rubbed her belly.

"Yes. We got plenty of water and supplies. Once I finish this window, we will be ready to ride out the storm. I still think we should go to the doc's or the plantation, so we can all be together."

"I just want to stay here. I feel comfortable here at our home."

"I know, but it just worries me." Trent said as he wrapped his arms around her.

"I will be fine. I am not due for another few weeks. I still have things to do to get ready for the baby to come. I am still sewing blankets and bonnets."

"What are you going to do when this baby turns out to be a boy?" Trent laughed.

"Well he can wear the bonnets, he won't know no better." She laughed.

Shaking his head, Trent opened the door and lead her from the porch, "You sit down and put your feet up. I will make you some broth."

Daisy did as she he said. She was feeling better today. This pregnancy had been a long one. She was ready for the baby to get here so she would feel like her old self again. She felt like a whale these days. Hobbling around with a huge belly was getting to be a nuisance. Daisy was nervous about the storm, but she did not want to go anywhere else, especially while she was pregnant. She was tired of the rough ride on the wagon. She just wanted to stay put, hunker down, and just enjoy being with Trent. She just prayed that this storm was not as bad as everyone thought it was going to be. Those dark clouds coming in looked ominous.

They both looked at each other as the first raindrops began to fall. It was almost relaxing listening to them, until the thunder and lightning started. Daisy would feel the electricity in the air. It made her uneasy. She started to rethink staying at the cabin, but it was too late now.

"It is getting late. There is nothing we can do sitting up listening to it rain. You want to go to bed and try to get some sleep?" Trent asked as he washed the last cup in the sink.

"Yes, I am a little tired."

They made their way to the bed to get some sleep. They both knew that this storm was just rolling in and it will get a lot worse before it got better. They snuggled in for that night. They both had no clue what they would be facing, in the next few days. They just knew that they would need their rest, no matter what it was.

Trent woke up and knew immediately that he had a fever. The sweat on his forehead and the pounding in in his ears was almost unbearable. He eased up out of bed and made his way to the kitchen. His mouth felt dry, and he was thirsty. *This is all I need to right now. Daisy pregnant. We are here alone and now I am sick. Damn it. Storms coming in.* He would not dare take Daisy out into this storm to fetch the doctor. He did not want to leave her alone either. He made his way over to the table and sat down. He could feel the sweat trickle down his back. As he went to get up from the table, he felt the room sway and then blackness wrapped around him.

Daisy awoke startled. With all the windows boarded up, she was not sure if it was dark or light out. She did see the glow of a lantern through the doorway. She felt and knew that Trent was no longer in bed. As she got up and walked closer to the door, it was eerily quiet, except the sound of the rain, as it pelted on the roof. As she neared the kitchen, she saw Trent on the floor. She rushed over to him. As she touched his forehead, she felt the heat. She rose, wet the hem of her gown, and rubbed his face in hopes of cooling him down to awaken him. He did not stir. She frantically looked around the room. She knew that she could not move him herself. She started to cry, "Trent please wake up! Please!" She laid her head on his chest. She could hear his breath and feel his heart beating on her cheek. She knew they both were in trouble. *I should have listened to him. We should not have stayed here alone. Oh, why did I not listen to him?*

Chapter 18
Twister

Faith awoke to a sound she had not heard since she was a child. She knew what it was a tornado, the moment she heard the howl. A sound one never forgets. She yelped as she heard debris hit the front of the cabin and heard glass break. Thankfully, the boards were in place and held out.

She looked over at the two huge men, who were scratching their heads in sleepy confusion. "Quickly! We need to get under the stairs; there is a hatch there with a little door that goes below in case the roof does not hold." Faith yelled.

They all three made their way to the stairs, pulled up the hatch to a small room and went below. There were numerous stairs went under the house into a small room. In the room, Faith lit a lantern. They closed the hatch and bolted the door from the inside. It was eerily quiet, with the occasional sound from above.

"I found this place a few days ago, when I was cleaning the cabin." Faith said as they all were sitting in the room. The room was small with benches along two sidewalls and a row of shelves was on the third wall adjacent to the door filled with goods. Faith did not know how old the supplies were, as Vayne never mentioned this room, but he had really made sure it had supplies. The sounds outside seem further away, as they were well insulated under the stairs.

Louis heard the sound and braced himself in the hole under the house. His heart was racing. He did not know if he was safe or should make a run for it. He decided to stay put. His ears popped from the pressure from the sudden change in the atmosphere. It sounded like an animal coming to attack him for all his evil deeds. He knew he deserved whatever the heavens may throw at him. He felt that he deserved to die. If he were not such a coward, he would look forward to dying and taken into oblivion. The whistling of the tornado and the debris that he saw through the hold, from underneath the house, reminded him of how vulnerable he really was.

The water starting seeping in gradually at first. The dirt began to shift and move and then the water rolled into the hole and like a river draining into the small space. Louis knew that he had a decision to make. It was either die or crawl out. He chose the latter.

Louis started to slide toward the opening. He felt as if he was in pudding, the mud was becoming so thick. He tried to crawl, but with nothing to hold on to, it was a feat. He finally reached the entrance and was able to grasp the side of the opening in the door, hoisted himself forward and was half in and half out of the hole under the cabin. As he pulled his legs up out of the muck, he felt his boots come off his feet. *Just great. I have lost my damn boots and now I do not have anything to protect my feet.* His mind was racing as he finally climbed from beneath the cabin. He struggled to stand up, as his legs had lost circulation from being restricted underneath the cabin. His stomach moaned. He has not eaten in hours, days, he could not remember. The rain pelted down from the heavens. He imagined if hell fury were in the form of water, this would be it. He knew that he was going to have to find a way to get into the cabin. He also knew that Faith was in that cabin, and this was not going to go well. The last time he saw her, was not pleasant. The things he did to her were damaging and evil. He knew this. He did not know how he would look at her or even explain him, as he could not understand why he did it himself. If she killed him, he would not blame her. He made his way to the porch. He kept close to the cabin, so he could hold on, as the wind was a beast. He could not see anything in the cabin. As he climbed up on to the porch. He took a breath and then knocked on the cabin door.

Chapter 19
The Clash

Faith, Slade and Benoit heard it at the same time. It was a muffled tap, tap, tap. They all just looked at each other. No one moved. They all heard it again, tap, tap, tap.

Faith raised a brow, "Is that someone knocking or is that noise from the storm?"

Both men looked at each other, back at Faith, and shrugged.

Slade rubbed his stubble, "Vayne is not due back yet. It must be from the storm."

Benoit shook his head in agreement.

They heard a noise again, but this time it was louder, more like a thump, thump, thump.

All three froze and looked at each other again.

Slade stood up, "There is only one way to find out." He unlatched the door, walked out, and stopped to listen again. Thump, thump, thump. "I'm coming, hold your horses!"

Slade stomped to the door, pulled up the latch and opened the door so quickly that Louis took a step back, startled.

"Can I help you?" Slade tilted his head to see.

"I, I, I need to come in out of the storm. I have been trapped out of here." Louis stammered.

"Who the hell are you? I know everyone on this island, and you are not one of them."

"My name is, uh," Louis swallowed hard.

"Well go ahead and spit it out. I need to get this door bolted back up." Slade snapped.

"I am Louis, Faith's cousin."

"Oh, well why you didn't just say so. Come on in." Slade had no idea who he was or what Louis had done.

Louis walked in slowly and looked around. He did not know what to do with himself.

"Well, C'mon, we have to go into the room under the stairs, so we can wait out this storm," Slade said.

"No that is okay. I am fine out here. I do not need to go anywhere. Besides, the tornado has dissipated. It left as quickly as it came."

Slade looked out the door, and he did not hear the whistling anymore. The rain was pouring, but the howling was gone. "You are right. I will be right back."

With this, Slade walked over and told Faith and Benoit it was safe to come out of the room.

Benoit came out and stretched and Faith followed. She was smiling, looking at Slade, when he shifted, and she caught sight of Louis. Slade noticed the smile left her face and the color with it.

"Miss Faith you okay? You are pale. Are you ill?"

"No, I am not ill." She walked past him and walked toward Louis. Both Slade and Benoit were startled when the sound rang out through the cabin. Faith punched Louis square in his nose and was on top of him before anyone knew what was happening. Louis was on his back, in the floor and Faith was pelting him with her fist.

Slade and Benoit could only stand there with my eyes wide and watched in amazement as she destroyed her cousin.

Slade reached down and touched her shoulder and she jumped startled. "Miss Faith, how about you let him up before you kill him and tell me what is going on." It was more of a statement than an actual question.

Faith slowly got to her feet and backed away. Tears ran down her cheeks. "I will be back." With that, she backed away and toward the stairs. When she was halfway up the stairs, she turned and said, "Get him tied up somewhere. I don't care where, just get him tied up."

Both men just looked at each other confused. They did as she said. They picked Louis up off the floor, placed him on the wooden chair across from the fireplace, in the corner. Tied him up and looked at him in amazement.

"I do believe she broke his nose," Benoit said and laughed.

Slade chuckled, "I do believe you are right."

Faith made it to the room and just collapsed on the bed. *How dare he show his face here? What is he doing here? How did he get here? Why did he not fight me back? It was probably because Benoit and Slade were there. This makes no sense. How did he make it here, all the way from Edwardstown? Had he been here this entire time? Vayne will kill him. I want to kill him. I will kill him.*

Faith got herself together and made her way back down the stairs. She walked toward Louis, and he flinched when she pulled up a chair in front of him.

"Don't worry; I am not going to hit you again, yet. How did you get here?" She asked.

"I hid on the ship, when it left Edwardstown."

"Why did you come here?" Faith leaned in closer.

"I honestly do not know Faith. I escaped the wagon, when the sheriff was taking me to town, but I could not remember anything. I just recently remembered what all I did to you." He put his head down.

Faith sat back and laughed. "You really expect me to believe that you did not remember what you did to me? What you did to your own mother?"

"I don't expect you to believe anything that I say. I don't even expect you to ever forgive me, but I am truly sorry Faith."

Faith blinked, "What is wrong with you? Did the statue hit you that hard and knock sense into you?"

"Faith, I do not know. I am not sure. I just know that I feel so much guilt that I would not blame you for putting a bullet through my head right now. Right between the eyes. I would be better off."

"I don't believe you." Faith said and examined is eyes. There seems to be something different there, but she knew that a leopard does not change his spots.

"I don't blame you for not believing me. What kind of a person does the things I now remember doing?" Louis said sobbing.

Faith was taken aback by is behavior.

"Faith I saw something. A spirit, ghost or whatever you want to call it. I know I was not dreaming, but she showed me. She made me feel the pain I had caused others. She made me see what I did. I was awake and saw these things. I am not lying. She was a Native American and told me she was going to let me see and feel what I have done. I felt it all."

Faith sat back and knew he was not lying. She had saw Ebony on several occasions. She knew that Ebony was watching out for her and Vayne. She knew that Ebony would have no issues visiting Louis. Faith could feel the truthfulness in his voice, and she could feel it in his energy at this moment.

"I believe you." Faith said.

Shocked, Louis said, "You do?"

"Yes, I do."

"This does not mean that I can stand the sight of you or that I want you in my presence. Nevertheless, yes, I believe you. I will figure out what to do when Vayne comes back."

Louis was relieved and then terrified when he thought about what Vayne would do to him.

Slade and Benoit sat and just listened. They did not know what he had done, but they knew it must have been bad. They would make sure to keep Faith safe until Vayne got back. They knew, from what they just witnessed, that Miss Faith might be small, but she can manage herself.

"You hungry?" Slade asked Louis.

"I am famished."

"Can you eat with your hands tied in front of you?"

"Yes I can." Louis would have ate it off the floor at this point. He was starving.

Slade tossed him a biscuit and Louis caught it and bit into it like a wild animal. Benoit brought him a ladle of water and put it to his lips so he could drink.

"How long you been here?" Benoit asked, taking a bite of a biscuit himself.

"Since the shipped docked when Faith came here." Louis said in between chews.

"Was that you in the lighthouse, when we were out there, before the storm came in?" Slade asked.

"That was me. I was staying there until the night you guys came out and I made a run for it."

"Where did you go after you fled the light house?" Slade snickered.

"I hid in a hole under the cabin."

Benoit chuckled, "I bet that was a sight to see. Wallowing around under the cabin, with the animals." He slapped his knee and laughed at his own joke.

Slade laughed and said, "Benoit here has kind of a sick sense of humor over somethings."

"I do not mind. I would rather be in here out of the weather than to be stuck out there anymore. I have never been an outside kind of man. I would rather be inside and clean. I cannot believe where my life is right now. I just cannot believe it." Louis shook his head.

Slade looked at Louis, "Things have a way of working themselves out. We all have done things. I do not know what you did or have done, but the way I see it, if you are sorry for your actions and want to do better, you can do better. If you genuinely want to be better, you must start over. You can make things right, eventually."

"I do not know about that. What I did was unforgiveable."

"That may be the case. You can still forgive yourself. That is one thing you can count on."

With that, Slade got up, lit another lantern, and stoked the fire.

Chapter 20
Land Ahoy

Land ho! All hand hoy! Vayne yelled as he spotted land through the spyglass. He was relieved that they made it out of the storm in one piece. The storm was rough, but the Lady Ebony handled it like a lady, as usual. The men rushed to deck. They were ready to get off the ship, visit the women in town, and enjoy the rum.

As the land got closer, Vayne gave orders, "All hands get ready to handle the gangplank. Ready the kellick. Great job Hearties. When we get to shore, I know in a few hours you all will be three sheets to the wind." Vayne grinned. "I know you all will be on the hunt for a wench also. I am ready to get back home to mine. Yo, ho, ho! We are ready to dock" The men cheered and sang as they readied the ship, so that they could depart and go partake in the festivities.

Vayne headed straight to Edwards Plantation. He knew it would take him a bit, since he did not have his horse and was walking, but that was okay, he needed to get rid of his sea legs. He was happy to be back but missed his wife. Everywhere he looked reminded him of her. He passed the creek where they met and could see Edwards Plantation in the distance. He forgot how beautiful it was here. The fields of wildflowers and green grass. The smell of honeysuckle hit is nose and smelled so sweet, made his mouth water. He closed his eyes and took the smell in. It made him homesick. He could not wait to get back to the cabin on the island. He was glad that he and Faith would split their time between the Island and the plantation.

He smiled as he saw Maw Sally sitting on the porch. Her dark head, wrapped in her usual scarf. She was rocking and humming a familiar tune. She squealed when she saw him.

"My sweet grandson is home! I have missed you!" Maw Sally hugged him tightly.

"I have missed you!" Vayne said as he picked her up and twirled her around.

"Faith did not make the trip?" Maw Sally asked.

"No Ma'am. Not this time." She is missing all of you.

"How is the dear child doing?"

"She is doing just fine. She loves the island, but she will be glad to get back to the mainland to see all of you." Vayne smiled.

John Edwards walked out of the door and handed Vayne a flask. "I know you need this after that voyage. This storm was a big one, but we fared well. No damage."

Vayne took the flask, "Yes, it was a rough out in open waters, but we fared well. The Lady Ebony is a strong ole girl. She did her job and the mates, and I did our part, to help her."

"I am glad to hear it. I was worried. I hope Faith faired okay." John looked concerned.

"I left her good hands with two of my mates, Slade and Benoit."

"I am glad to hear that. I knew you would make sure she was safe." John said as he took a drink and leaned his head back on the rocker. "How long are you staying with us?"

"I will be here for a few days to get stocked up on supplies to take back to the island. Have they found Louis yet? Vayne asked through gritted teeth.

"No one has seen him. We do not know if he is dead or alive. We have no clue where he is. The sheriff has not seen hide nor hair of him either." John breathed out and shook his head.

Vayne shook his head, "Well, he will show up if he is alive."

Mas Sally did not comment, but just shook her head and went back to humming.

"How is Trent and Daisy?"

"We saw them a while back, and they were doing well. Daisy is big with child." John said.

"I will ride out to see them sometime while I am here. We have catching up to do I may see if Trent needs any help while I am here." Vayne said.

As they were talking, Ms. Alma came out the screen door with a big grin, "Vayne! Oh, we have missed you!"

Vayne stood and gave her a big hug. "We have missed you to. How is the bookstore?"

"It's the same. I am about ready to give it up. I am getting too old to be on my feet so much."

Vayne just smiled, as he knew there was no right answer to that remark. Never comment on a woman's age or weight.

Vayne stood up and asked, "Maw Sally and Ms. Alma I need to speak to you both, if you don't mind."

Maw Sally and Miss Ida followed Vayne into the house. Once inside they sat at the dining room table. Maw Sally made cups of coffee for all three of them. Both women sat and stared at him in anticipation. Both were thinking that Faith is with child, but they did not want to ask.

"Maw Sally, I saw mama. I know you think I am ridiculous, but I saw her." Vayne stated, eye staring intently.

Maw Sally smiled, "I believe you. I heard her. She called me Agitsi. That means mother in our native language. She sees you to, and she is proud of you."

Vayne felt a tear slide down his cheek and brushed it away. "Ms. Alma, Al was not my father."

Ms. Alma's eyes opened wide, "How do you know?"

"My mother Ebony told me when she came to me. My father was a Warrior." Vayne said as he watched her. He did not want her to be upset and felt a little guilty about his relief.

"I am so glad you found this out Vayne." Alma said.

"You are?" Vayne was surprised.

"Yes, I would not want you to live thinking that your father was such a terrible person, and you were conceived that way." Ida wiped a tear.

Vayne hugged her, "I was conceived in love by my parents. Mother showed me. She showed me my father."

Maw Sally stood up, walked around the table, and hugged him. She knew he was right, she felt it. As she looked up, she glanced over and saw the butterfly again. It was sitting in the window, as if to watch them. Maw Sally gave it a wink, as she knew that was a sign her Ebony was watching this moment.

Chapter 21
Seeing Doubles

Vayne got up early the next morning and started to make his way to see Trent and Daisy, at the cabin. The smells of the ocean, mixed with the wildflowers and honeysuckle was a welcome enjoyment to his nostrils. He noticed the birds singing, and the colors are more vibrant. He was not sure if it was his mood, or he just never stopped to notice it before. He felt lighter today. He missed his wife, but he felt as if he could fly. The heaviness of the last year felt as if it had left his shoulders. He now knows who his father was. He was made by love and not some violent act is mother had to endure. He never really knew how much this weighed on him, until he no longer had to carry that burden.

Vayne arrived at the cabin and tethered his horse. It was quiet. He knocked on the door lightly and heard stirring on the inside, then someone crying.

"Trent? Daisy? Anyone here?"

Daisy heard the knock and recognized his voice. "Vayne! Help me!"

Vayne tried to open the door but could not get it to budge. "Daisy, I cannot open the door."

Daisy wailed, "It is secured, and I have not been able to get it open."

"Step away from the door and make sure all is clear. I will get it open from the outside."

Vayne stepped back on the porch and kicked the door. It made a sound but did not open. He kicked the door a second time, and it flew open with splinters scattering the floor. Vayne saw Daisy on the floor by Trent.

Vayne rushed over, "Is he okay? Are you okay? What happened?"

Daisy through tears, "I do not know. He has been like this a few days, I think, and I have been unable to move him. He is burning up. I have managed to get water down him. I could not get the door open to fetch help. I have been having pain in my belly."

Vayne glanced at Daisy and was amazed at how big she was with child. "Daisy, you go lay down. I am going to get him up and get the wagon hitched. You both are going back to the plantation with me."

Daisy did not argue and went to lay down and wait on Vayne to finish. She knew that she would not argue with him. If she should have listened to Trent to begin with and they would not have been in this situation to begin with. She was so relieved to see their old friend. As she was getting comfortable on the bed, the pain hit her. She had never felt pain like this and somehow, she knew that when they left this cabin, she would not be pregnant any longer. She gritted her teeth and struggled to sit up. She was able to get off the side of the bed and turn to place her elbows on the bed, while she struggled to take off her undergarments. She had the urge to push. All she wanted to do was push.

Vayne got the wagon and got the horses hooked up. He picked Trent up and got him onto the rug in front of the fireplace when he heard Daisy.

"Vayne! I need your help." Daisy said loudly, but calmly.

Vayne rushed to the room and saw her, "What do you need me to do. Do you need help getting on the bed?"

Daisy became strangely calm. She was sweating. "No. I do not need you to help me on the bed. I need you to help me have a baby."

Vayne backed up and put up his hands, "No, No, No. You need to hold out until we get to the Mr. Edwards. Ms. Alma and Maw Sally is there. They will know what to do. "

"Vayne Lafitte, I have no control over that. We do not control when this baby wants to make an entrance, so you buck up and get some water." Daisy looked him in the eye.

"Yes ma'am. You sure you cannot hold out?"

Her look said it all, and he just backed out of the room and went to heat water. He was lucky, there was already a kettle over the fire.

Daisy was trying to push when Vayne made it back to the room. Vayne felt his stomach turn but managed to compose himself.

"Daisy, what do I do? I have never delivered a baby before."

"You just stand there and support my back. I will do all the work. I have never done this either, but I was always told a woman's body knows what to do. Let us just pray mine does."

Daisy grunted and pushed, "Get down and catch the baby. I cannot do that part. Get that blanket over there and get it ready. I feel it coming!"

Vayne grabbed the blanket and knelt down. Daisy still had her dress on, and Vayne was thankful for that, as all he could see was the back of her dress.

"Here he comes," Daisy said.

Vayne felt the little bundle hit his hand. "It's a boy!"

"Rub his stomach and clean his nose and mouth out." Daisy said.

Vayne did this and the squeal that Vayne heard made him smile. It reminded him of the baby piglets he watched being born when he was a child. He felt tears burn his eyes. He thought of how Trent would feel when he got better and knew he missed this.

"Oh no!" Daisy started to grunt again.

"What is wrong? What do I need to do?" Vayne said standing up.

"I think there is another one."

"Another one? What do you mean another one? Another baby?" Vayne asked.

Daisy turned her head to the side and said, "No a puppy. What do you think I mean?"

Vayne was in disbelief. He gently laid the baby down in the hollowed-out log, that he knew Trent had built. He picked up the other blanket, knelt as he did the first time, and felt the second bundle fall in his hands. "It's a girl." Vayne knew from the first one to rub her stomach and clean out her nose and mouth. Vayne was in awe of these two babies and the way Daisy had handled this situation.

"Are there anymore?" he asked.

"I hope and pray not. This is a surprise. Help me onto the bed and bring me the hot water so that I can get cleaned up."

Vayne turned to get the water and turned just in time to see Daisy pick the little boy up and put him to her breast. He turned to give her privacy and then he looked down at the little girl in his arms and smiled. She was sucking on her hands.

"I think she is hungry." He reached and handed her to Daisy.

Daisy placed her on the other breast and began to feed both babies instinctively.

"Do you need me to do anything else? If not, I will check on Trent and once we make sure you are okay, we can try to get to the plantation." Vayne could not stop looking at those two little bundles so helpless.

"I am good. Go check on Trent and make sure he is okay, and I will sit for a spell and make sure I am good to go. I don't feel any pain, and all feels okay."

As he was walking away, he heard Daisy call his name. He turned, "Yes maam?"

"Thank you, Vayne. You did an excellent job. I could not have done it without you."

"My pleasure ma'am. You managed yourself like only a woman could." He tipped the brim of his hat.

"I have helped deliver a few babies at the brothel. Although, never more than one at a time. That was quite a surprise." Daisy smilles.

"Well, you did a mighty fine job." Vayne said, as he exited the room.

As Vayne exited the room, he saw Trent stirring. He helped Trent to sit up. He felt of his head and noticed that his head was cool to the touch.

"Looks like your fever is going down. If you wanted to get out of all the work, all you had to do was say so." Vayne smirked.

Trent looked around confused. "I have been out of it. I took sick."

"I would say you have been out of it. Your wife can manage business when you are not awake to take up the slack." Vayne laughed.

The sound of the babies crying had both men looking at the door to the bedroom, where Daisy was.

"What is that?" Trent looked confused.

"Well, that would be your son and daughter. Seems they are finished eating."

Trent looked from the door to Vayne and back at the door, "You mean...?"

"Yes, and I suggest you get in there to meet them." Vayne held out his hand to help him stand.

"I will give you two some privacy and get things loaded. I am taking you all back to Edwards. You both will need help for a while, with two babies. Plus, I would like all of us to spend time together," Vayne said over his shoulder walking away.

Trent made his way to the door and caught his breath as he saw Daisy holding the babies. He walked over to the bed and choked back tears. "I missed the birth. I am so sorry." He laid his head on the bed near her.

Daisy reached down and rubbed his head, "Do not you fret. Vayne handled it like a champion. You were sick and were in no shape to help anyone."

"Vayne! Well, who would have thought he had it in him! A boy and a girl. I cannot believe it. Two of them. I did not want to say anything, but I thought you looked big, and now I know why. You were carrying two. Two! What are we going to do with two of them?" Trent was wide-eyed.

"Well, we are going to love them, raise them. What else would we do?" Daisy laughed.

"I am in shock. What are we going to name them?" Trent rubbed his chin. "We were not thinking of having to name two."

Daisy called for Vayne, and he entered the doorway. "What is your middle name Vayne."

Vayne raised a brown, "Vayne."

Daisy laughed, "Well what is your middle name then?"

"Jean (SZ-Ahhn-N) Vayne Lafitte, is my full name."

"Trent meet your son named, Jean (SZ-Ahhn-N)." Daisy handed him to Trent.

"I am honored Daisy. I am truly honored." Vayne bowed.

"This little girl here will be Rose. We will call her Rosie."

Trent smiled big, "I like that. Our little Rose and my wife Daisy. Vayne, I cannot thank you enough. I do not know what to say. Thank you sounds so insufficient."

"No thank you needed. I am sure you would have done the same thing, had it been Faith. You are my brother. We may not be brothers by blood, but you are my brother. You are my best friend. This is what we do."

With this, Trent stood, and the two men hugged. Vayne slapped him on the back. "Let us get everyone loaded up. I cannot wait to see all of their faces when we get there with two babies. Especially when we were not expecting them yet! They might have come early, but they are healthy from the looks of it!"

Chapter 22
Discussions

Vayne, Trent, Daisy and the babies arrived at the plantation later that same evening. Trent drove the wagon with Daisy and the babies and drove slowly, as to not jostle Daisy or the babies. Vayne rode beside him, and they all talked on the way. It was a pleasant ride, but Daisy was relieved when the house came into view. Maw Sally was sitting in her usual spot on the porch, along with Ms. Alama, as she lived there now. Vayne tethered his horse and went around assisting Trent with Daisy and the babies. Maw Sally was watching from the porch and jumped up when she saw Trent hand Vayne, not one but two little bundles of joy.

"Lord have mercy! What do we have here?" Maw Sally asked as she walked to Vayne with her arms held out. "Give me that precious baby. Wait. There are two of them! Ms. Alma, come quick and look at this! Ms. Daisy has done gone had us two to spoil!"

Daisy climbed down from the wagon, with the assistance of the two men, "Maw Sally and Ms. Alma, I would like you both to meet Jean (SZ-Ahhn-N) and Rose. With Vayne's assistance, they made their entrance into the world this morning."

The two women looked at each other and smiled. They were not interested in the details; they just wanted to sit and rock the sweet babies.

"It has been years since we have had a baby around. I am going to enjoy this." Ms. Alma said.

"Oh yes, we are, Ms. Alma. We will spoil them rotten." Maw Sally said and started humming.

Vayne recognized her little tune. It brought back memories he had not thought of in years.

John Edwards came out of the screen door. "Well, I will be. What do we have here? Oh, two of them. I never saw that coming."

Maw Sally smiled, "I did. I knew she had to be carrying twins, or I was hoping she was. Ms. Daisy has a small frame, and I knew something was up."

"Well, I am feeling much better now. It all happened so fast, and I feel like I could run a marathon now. I can breathe again. I have felt bad for so long, I forgot how good I felt before I was pregnant. The delivery was so fast, and it was over before I knew it. The elders always said that a woman's body knows what to do. They were right."

Maw Sally shook her head, "That is true. Some women used to have babies in the fields and be back to work the next day. True story."

They all laughed and sat on the porch to enjoy the afternoon. The sun was high up in the sky, but it was a gentle breeze, which felt like butterfly wings against your skin. The babies enjoyed the rocking chairs just as much as the older women enjoyed rocking them.

John Edwards looked at Vayne, "When do you think you will be heading back to the island?"

"It will be a few days. I wanted to talk to all of you and see if you all wanted to go back to the island with me. Maw Sally, Ms. Alma, You, Trent, and Daisy. Faith has been missing everyone and would love to see all of you. It should be smooth sailing now that the storm has passed. I will wait until Daisy is feeling like her old self again, of course. I have never had any babies on my ship before, but The Lady Ebony has never let me down and I trust the old girl. I was thinking that we all could split time at the island and the plantation. All stay together. I know that Faith gets homesick, and I have grown quite fond of all of you, and you are my family as well. I just think it would be a good thing. Maybe spend the summer at the island and winters here. I have not discussed this in detail with Faith yet, but I know she would love it. What do you all think?"

Everyone looked at him and smiled. They all knew that they would love to go.

John was the first to speak up. "I will be glad to go. I have never been on a ship before, would be interesting. Maw Sally, Ms. Alma, are you all up for going?"

"They say old dogs don't learn new tricks, but I guess we can take our rockers and me and Ms. Alma can take the rocking chairs, right? We can learn how to rock on a ship."

"We can load the rockers and get you both a good spot," Vayne winked.

Ms. Alma fidgeted with her hands. "I don't know how to swim."

Vayne knelt, "Ms. Alma, it will be just fine. If anything happens, I will throw you a rope. I promise to be gentle if we must use it."

"I trust you dear boy. I trust you. I would love to come." Ms. Smiled and continued to rock the baby.

The next day, John started to get trunks packed and things organized in the house. He knew he had a lot to do before they left. Maw Sally was prepping food to take with them. She wanted to cook and pack Faith's favorite foods and deserts. She was in the kitchen when Vayne walked in. She immediately handed him a cup of coffee.

"Maw Sally, do you know of anything that Faith might be missing? I know she did not take all her belongings when we left." Vayne said as he took a sip of his coffee.

"You might want to pack some of her books and take to her. I am not sure if she took any, but if she did, I am sure she can always use more."

"That is a promising idea. I will get some of her books and get her some Castile soap and some other things. Thanks for the help, Maw Sally." Vayne reached down and gave her a kiss on top of the head.

"Ms. Alma do you need help at the store to get anything? I will glad to help you." Vayne turned to her at the table.

"I do believe I will need some assistance. I also have books that I think Faith would like to have. I need to getclothes and some proper shoes to take with me." She said.

"I will go with you into town. Just let me know when you are ready and I will hitch up a wagon, which will make it easier."

"I sure will." Ms. Alma went back to knitting. She was knitting blankets for the babies. She wanted to make a pink one and a blue one. She knew that Trent and Daisy were only expecting one baby. She wanted to help all that she could.

John came in from the den, "I spoke to Sampson, the supervisor, and he is going to keep things in order and running while we are away. He has his grandsons to help him also. I told them that they could all stay in the house if they would like to. I trust him. He is a good man."

Maw Sally smiled, "Yes, he is a good man. Been with us for years that one has. He comes from a good family. He will keep everything running smoothly. Did you talk to your employees at the bank?"

"I did and they all know the plans and they can handle it all while I am gone. I am really looking forward to seeing Faith. I have deeply missed her." John sighed.

"I have missed that child so much. It hurt my heart when she first left, but knowing she was happy, made it all okay."

Chapter 23
A Pirate Lost in Thought

Everyone was busy loading the ship. It was time to set sail and go back to the island. Vayne was happy. He knew how happy Faith would be that everyone was with them. He could not wait to see the look on her face when they all made it to the cabin. Since meeting Faith, he now understood the importance of the family bonds he had created. He also understood that family is not just about the blood ties that bind you, family was about the relationship and bonds of love.

He got Maw Sally and Ms. Alma settled with their rocking chairs and, of course, the babies on the ship. He had never had elderly women on the ship before or rocking chairs. He chuckled to himself. He would just make sure to keep her stead. He had strategically placed his men around. Just in case. John Edwards looked a bit out of place with his suit and tie. Vayne just shook his head. One thing he could say about John Edwards, he was who he was. He never denied or tried to hide it. He did think that John would enjoy assisting him with steering the ship. Being the captain of his own life, John was sure to enjoy this experience.

Vayne watched as Trent and Daisy stood together and embraced looking out toward the ocean. He wanted to talk to Trent and Daisy about staying and building a home on the island. He was sure that Daisy and Faith would love it.

He was not accustomed to what he was feeling these days. He has always been a loaner. He never wanted anything to hold him down. He knew that he was changing. He also knew that it was for the better. He longed for the family ties that he had. He longed for togetherness. He was alone for so many years, lost. He knew that Faith had reached a part of him that he never really knew was there. He had let his guard down and learned to trust.

His thoughts came back to Paddy. His old friend. He had not realized, until he lost Paddy, how close he had grown to the old geezer. It amazed him how losing someone can make you think about your own mortality. It can make you think about the years you have lost and make you want to live one day at a time. His heart still hurt to think of his old friend. Paddy was the closest thing he had ever had to a father.

It made him smile to just sit back and watch everyone. The smiles and laugher. It made him happy to hear the laughing and to see the babies. The babies that he helped to deliver. The babies that came early but were healthy. He just shook his head in awe. He was in no hurry. He just wanted to sit back and watch the people he loved. All in one place. The only person missing was Faith. When he arrived at the cabin, he knew she would be just as happy as he was now.

Faith had no clue that he longed for a baby as much as she did. He was at peace knowing that his mother could see them and know that he found love. He knew that his mother was always watching over them. Vayne also knew that he was in a season of life that he knew just how important the things were. He just hoped that all his loved ones could one day see things, as he sees them now.

He knew that his sailing days were gone. No more going to the open sees to take and give to others. He was finally ready to give that up. He would use, The Lady Ebony, for things like today. To get back and forth from the island to the mainland. To transport family and goods. His sneaky pirate days were behind him. Well, unless he was being sneaky to surprise his wife, which was an exception. He never thought he would be able to give that up. He never thought he would want to. He smiled again to himself; yes, he was ready, willing, and able.

Trent looked over and saw Vayne smiling, which was new to him. "What are you smiling like a Cheshire cat for?"

Vayne chuckled, "Nothing. I am happy. I cannot really explain it."

"I can explain it, old friend. You are content. Content is what I feel with Daisy. I notice everything now and am just, well content." Trent slapped him on the back and walked back to Daisy.

Vayne knew that his friend understood exactly how he felt. Trent was right. The word was content. Jean (SZ-Ahhn-N) Vayne Lafitte was finally content in his life.

Who in the hell would have thought it.

Chapter 24
Open Seas and Incoming Surprise

It was beautiful, blue clear skies as the ship left port. There were no clouds, and the seagulls were enjoying the clear weather. Diving, flying up, up, up, and then diving again. The Sea ducks were out and enjoying the beautiful weather. Maw Sally was in awe of them. She loved when they would diver under the water and then she had to guess where they would come back up. Ms. Alma laughed and was in awe of them. None of them had ever been out to sea before and watched in amazement at the marine life.

"The ducks do not go too far from shore. But I am sure we will see some dolphins during this journey." Vayne said. He was enjoying their excitement. He remembered how Faith reacted the first time she made this journey. She had the same joyful reaction.

As they went out further and land was no longer visible, the bottlenose dolphins showed up so that they could show off. John Edwards thought the Dolphins were magnificent. He had read about them but had never seen one with his own eyes.

Vayne explained, "There are varied species of dolphins in these waters. The bottlenose tends to stay nearer to shore than other species. The Bottlenose are my favorites. I call them the children of the sea. The remind me of children at play. They always look like they are smiling, and they are little show offs. They travel in pods. A pod is a group of dolphins. They hunt and play in pods. They are highly intelligent creatures."

As he said this, a team of two jumped and dove back down, as if they were showing the spectators what he was talking about and decided to give a demonstration. The women all clapped in unison, at the spectacle. They all watched the dolphins glide and spin through the water. They dolphins would stay with them most of trip, as if they were the welcoming committee.

The skies remained clear and blue all day. As nighttime fell, the entertainment did not end there. The crewmembers planned some musical entertainment. Everyone gathered around to listen.

Come all ye young fellow that follows the sea,
To me, way hey, glow the man down,
Now please pay attention and listen to me,
Give me some time to flow the man down.

The singing went late into the night, until everyone went to his or her prospective sleeping quarters and went to sleep. Today had been a good day.

The trip continued for a few more days and the island came into view. As they neared the island, the family watched as Vayne and his crew readied the ship to dock. It was obvious to all of the family that he knew exactly what he was doing and was very good at being a captain and they all knew he was a good leader, no matter what he did. They all were impressed with him and his men.

As they anchored offshore in the deeper waters, the men would move in closer and ground the boat at low tide. The men readied the dinghies, and everyone loaded on. The men would bring the cargo ashore. They headed toward the island and Vayne was so glad to be back.

Faith saw the ship, as it made its way toward the shore. The cabin was finally back in order, and she knew that when Vayne made it to the cabin, she would need to speak to him before he saw the Louis. She wanted him to be aware before he walked in and was shocked and angry. No good would come of that and she knew it. She felt butterflies in her stomach. Oh, how she had missed him.

"Vayne is back." She turned toward Slade and Benoit.

"Aye, we will walk down to meet him. He may need help if he is carrying anything." Benoit said as he headed toward the door. Slade followed him.

"Slade and Benoit please do not mention the visitor to him. I would like to speak to him myself."

The men looked at her, shook their heads in agreement, and grunted. They had no clue what this man had done, but it was more than the Faith would like to talk about.

The men made their way down to the beach and patted Vayne on the back.

"Welcome back. Glad to see your fared well with the storm." Slade said.

"Yes, we faired good. How is everything here? How is my wife?"

"All went well. We did not have severe damage, just debris but we got everything back in order quickly. The lighthouse did not sustain any damage, which is surprising." Benoit answered.

"Miss Faith is fine. She handled like a champ," Said Slade.

Vayne laughed, "I would not expect any less from her. She can handle herself."

Vayne made introductions to the family. "Faith does not know that I brought the entire family with me. She is going to be happy."

They all walked to trail toward the Cabin. Slade and Benoit assisted Ms. Alma and Maw Sally, as this was quite a walk for them. Daisy and Trent were behind everyone else, with the babies. John Edwards held the lead with Vayne. Both men were in a hurry to see Faith.

As the cabin came into view, John Edwards smiled. It was just as he has pictured, and he knew that Faith must love it here. As they approached the cabin, Faith squealed as saw both the men in her life that she loved.

"Father! What a surprise!" She leapt into his arms first. She turned to Vayne smiling and gave him a big hug. She caught sight of Maw Sally and Ms. Alma and her smile got even bigger.

"Maw Sally! Ms. Alma!" She hugged them tightly. Vayne just brought the entire house back with him.

"Well, almost all," Dolly said as she walked up. She was holing baby Rose and Trent was holding baby Jean.

Faith could not contain herself; she took baby Rose and just smiled at her. "Oh Daisy! You did so well. You had one of each and they are so adorable. What a wonderful day!"

"Let's get everyone inside," Vayne walked toward the door.

Faith's heart sank, "Oh wait! I need to speak to you. I did not realize everyone was coming, but before you go in, I must tell you..." She trailed off.

Vayne raised a brow and looked at her.

"Louis is inside."

Vayne's anger took over. "Did you just say that Louis was inside?"

"Yes but wait. Before you go in, I want you to calm down. He was on the ship when we arrived back from the mainland. We have him incapacitated now. I do not want you to kill him. I am not sure what happened to him, but he is different."

"Different!" Vayne yelled.

John Edwards walked toward Faith, "Honey, he is a dangerous man and must be dealt with as such."

"Father, I know this. It is really confusing and odd. I do not know what to make of it."

"Oh, I will get it out of him. I will see what is so different about the lowlife." Vayne stormed into the cabin.

Chapter 25
The Confrontation

Vayne walked into the cabin. He saw Louis and rounded the couch, as if to stalk his prey. Louis's eyes were big in fear. He had been dreading this moment. He knew that he deserved everything that he got.

"You have the nerve to show your face," Vayne walked toward him.

"I know that you want to kill me right now. I want to end it myself. What I did to Faith, my mother, to everyone, is inexcusable. I do not know if I will ever forgive myself."

Vayne tilted his head, "Who are you trying to convince? Me or yourself?"

Louis shook his head, "If I am being honest, probably both of us."

"What are you apologizing for? I want to hear you say it." Vayne took a seat a chair in front of Louis, so that they could be eye level. The other family had walked into the cabin and were watching the two from the kitchen.

"I am sorry for killing my own mother. I am sorry for hurting Faith, not once but multiple times, starting all the way from our childhood. I was always bad and had these feelings of wanting to hurt something. I do not know why I always felt that way. I am just a bad seed."

Vayne laughed, "A bad seed. You are evil and wretched."

Louis squirmed in the chair, "You are correct. I do not even know what has happened to me. I remember the statue hitting me at the house. I remember a gunshot. The next thing I remembered was waking up on the Sheriffs Wagon and knew that I was going to jail. I jumped off the back of the wagon and made a run for it. It took me a bit, to remember what I had done. The thing is, I felt terrible about what I had done. I had never experienced any remorse, prior to the incident.

I do not know what to make of this. In all honesty, I would prefer not having a conscience. A conscience makes you feel terrible."

"So, you expect all of us to believe that you have turned over a new leaf. That a bump on the head has made you into this new person?" Vayne shook his head in disgust, "I should just kill you right now, or make you walk the plank."

"I would not blame you for anything you do to me. Do as you wish." Louis said and closed his eyes.

Vayne pulled out his knife and put it to Louis's throat, Faith and the family looked on. Faith moved closer to Vayne and put her hand on his shoulder, "Please do not. No good could come of it. There has been too much hate all these years. It does not solve anything. I am not saying he does not need to be punished, but it needs to be handed down by the sheriff and done the right way."

"He hurt you, Faith."

"I am fine now. What he did was despicable, but he is sick. He is sick in the head. We cannot help him. Killing him will not help you. Hand me the knife Vayne. Please." Faith spoke calmly and Vayne loosened his grip on the knife and let her take it. She sat the knife down, wrapped her arms around her husband, and held him close. She could feel his heartbeat on her chest. She felt it slowing down and knew that he was calming. He had death in his eyes and when she pulled back and looked at her, all she saw now was love.

"I will get him to the ship and order the men to take him back to Edwardstown so that the sheriff can deal with him. I will tell the men to make sure no harm comes to him. Slade and Benoit get him to the ship. Tell the men once they get the cargo and personal trunks for the family off the ship, head back to Edwardstown and deliver him. I will not go on this voyage; my men can manage themselves."

Slade and Benoit walked over to Louis and pulled him from the chair, "C'mon, you have a voyage to make back to the mainland." Slade said, taking him from the cabin by the arm.

As Louis was going out of the door, he looked back and said, "I really am sorry about everything."

Faith did not respond to him, except to nod her head at him and then the door closed. As the door closed, Faith smiled to herself, because the symbolism of the door was not lost on her. She had closed that chapter of her life. The anger and pain left, with Louis.

Chapter 26
Family

Things settled down the next few days. They all discussed spending time between the island and the mainland. Trent and Daisy decided to take Vayne up on his offer to live on the Island. Maw Sally and Ms. Alma, to Faith's surprise, wanted to stay also. Faith laughed when Maw Sally said that she was an old dog and could learn new tricks. John Edwards said he would like to spend time between the island and the plantation; no one blames him for that. They all would go back and forth, as they chose. Faith knew that he home would always be on the island, however, she would visit the plantation also. It would always be her home as well.

Trent and Daisy walked in with the babies, "Vayne and Faith, we want to speak to you both."

Vayne and Faith walked over, and each took a baby, "We would like to ask you both to be the babies God Parents. In case something happened to us, we would like to know that you would take care of them."

Faith and Vayne glanced at one another; both agreed that it would be an honor for them.

Both Vayne and Faith had grown quite fond of little rose and Jean. Jean's name was still awe-inspiring to Faith. She thought it was a beautiful gesture. She was also still in shock that her husband has helped deliver two babies. Her husband was just full of surprises.

The seasons slowly changed on the island and trips back and forth to the mainland were a regular occurrence. Trent and Daisy finally finished building their cabin with room enough for more children if they so decided to have. Vayne has built on to the cabin and added Maw

Sally and Ms. Alma their own rooms downstairs. He knew that the two elderly women did not need to go up and down the stairs. He also knew that when he and Faith had children, they would be upstairs with them. They were getting to practice on Jean and little Rosie, so by the time they had children, they would be highly trained in the taking care of little ones. It was a pleasure having the babies around.

John Edwards had gone back to the plantation a few weeks ago to check in with the bank and the house. He had made a few trips back and forth. He will spend a month on the mainland and two weeks on the island. He and Vayne had worked out the schedule so that Vayne could send the men, when the time came to go pick him up. John Edwards was becoming quite the captain as Vayne gave men orders to let him steer the ship and supervise John.

The island was now well-stocked with cattle, sheep, horses, goats, and chickens. They even had a dairy cow that they placed close to the cabin. Slade and Benoit had their parcels across the island, and they all pitched in and got the land fenced off. The island was becoming productive. The gardens were flourishing, as they found a freshwater spring up hill, which meant irrigation was easy, and getting that water to the gardens was imperative, and with the flow going downhill, that was an extremely easy task and Vayne was pleasantly surprised. The lighthouse was finished and able to shine the light of hope to all who passed by. The last visit from John Edwards gave great news regarding Louis. The Sheriff received him alive and well. Louis was now a permanent resident the asylum. Faith read years ago, that some of the treatment in these facilities were cruel, but that was out of her control. He was where he needed to be.

As the days passed by, Faith wondered if she would ever be with child. She knew, her not being pregnant, was not from lack of trying. She knew that it would happen at the right time. She was really enjoying everyone on the island. Maw Sally and Ms. Alma were relaxed and happy.

"Maw Sally, can I ask you a question? Faith sat down next to her.

"Child you can ask me anything," Maw Sally answered.

"Do you think there is a reason I have not gotten with child yet?" Faith asked shyly.

"Oh child, it will happen when the good Lord sees fit for it to."

"I think so to, but I just figured I would have conceived by now," Faith said.

Maw Sally smiled, "Sometimes when we stop worrying about things that is when they happen child."

Faith knew she was right. She needed to stop trying so hard and thinking about it and just be happy and it would happen eventually.

Daisy walked onto the porch and handed Faith Rosie, "Do you mind watching her so I can go and soak in the stream for a bit?"

"Of course I don't mind," Faith said as she bounced Rosie on her knee.

"Jean is with Trent, at the cabin. I will not be long.

Daisy said over her shoulder.

"Take your time. Come on little Rosie, let us go walking."

As Faith was walking toward the lighthouse, she felt the familiar feeling of Ebony. She knew she was near. "Hello Miss Ebony. I am starting to recognize your presence. "

As she entered the lighthouse, she saw Ebony appear. She smiled at Faith. She spoke without moving her lips. "Do not worry Faith. You and my son will have children. You will prosper and multiply."

Faith felt tears slide down her cheeks. "Thank you, Ebony. I am so thankful that we have you watching over us. God must have made you an angel."

"I am no angel, but God is happy with me. You love my son, so I love you, my daughter. You will think of me each time you see this lighthouse. I am always with you and the light that shines as a symbol of hope." Ebony said as she faded out of sight.

"Did you see and hear that little Rosie?"

Rosie was looking in the direction where Ebony came and vanished, she started smiling and laughing. "I knew you could sense her to. You smart girl you. Let's go home. I am sure your mommy is back by now."

Daisy was back at the cabin by the time Faith and Rosie made it back. The entire family was sitting on the porch, including Vayne. It had become an afternoon ritual, to sit on the porch, talk and sing old hymns. Sometimes Maw Sally would sing the songs of her tribes. Vayne and Faith had grown to look forward to the afternoon. They were enjoying everyone being together. It was quite relaxing. As it got later, everyone went to their perspective places and homes, Vayne, and Faith made their way upstairs to get some rest.

Vayne picked up Faith, surprised her, and took her upstairs. "Are we ready to go to bed Mrs. Lafitte?"

"I believe I am, Mr. Lafitte." Faith giggled.

As they entered the bedroom, Vayne eased her down slowly and kissed her gently on the lips. "I really do love you. You know that?" He said as he smiled.

Faith still got butterflies, "I do know you love me, and I know you know that I love and adore you. You are my world. I do not know what I would do without you." She kissed him back.

"Well, you will not have to worry about being without me. I am yours and you are mine. I am so glad you are my wife." Vayne slipped her dress over her head, they got into bed, they both let the love intermingle between them, and they both knew that nothing would ever be able to come between them. They were now one.

Vayne got up early the next morning and went to check on the livestock and get the eggs, so that Faith would have fresh ones when she came down. As he finished feeding the livestock, he walked to the chickens and as he made it to the coop, his mother Ebony appeared in front of him.

"Mother, I sometimes get worried when you come to me." Vayne said.

"Do not be afraid, I am always with you. You just do not always see me. You and Faith will have children. I know you both long for it. It will happen in God's timing."

Vayne went to speak, and she was gone. *How did she know that was on my mind?*

Vayne finished gathering the eggs, and then he milked the cow and headed back to the house. He was lost in thought as he entered the house. He was startled, he did not see Maw Sally before she spoke to him, "I got a penny for your thoughts."

"Oh I am not really thinking of anything in particular. Simply happy I guess." He said.

Maw Sally smiled, "Have you noticed a certain glow about Faith here lately?"

Vayne looked puzzled, "She is always beautiful to me."

Maw Sally just nodded and went out onto the porch to perch in her rocking chair and knit. Vayne just shook his head as she walked off. *She is getting senile in her old age.* Vayne laughed and went outside to do some more chores.

Chapter 27
Pitter Patter

The spring turned into summer and the summer turned into fall. It was beautiful on the island. The rosemary was blooming, there were purples, greens, and yellows. The colors were never ending, but the orange and yellow leaves on the surrounding trees were more beautiful than anything Faith had ever seen. She was in awe daily of the gems she found on this island. Whether it be trees or flowers, that she did not know the names of, she was forever amazed.

Jean and little Rosie were walking now, and they all chased them around the island barefoot. They had the energy of a stallion. Faith was chasing Jean when she felt the dizziness take over. She caught up to him but was out of breath when she reached him. She picked him up and took him to Daisy.

"I am going to go inside and lay down for a bit. I am feeling winded today. I did not get enough sleep last night." Faith said as she handed Jean to Daisy.

Vayne was walking toward the cabin from the trail. He had been down at the beach casting a line to see if he could catch fish for supper. He realized that fishing is one of his favorite hobbies now. After he had caught some for supper. He saw Faith as she went inside. As he approached Daisy, he gave Jean a high five.

"I am going to take these in to see if Faith wants to cook these up for supper," He showed his catch to Daisy.

"I do not think Faith is feeling well. She said she was going inside to lay down for a bit." Daisy said as she was trying to get Jean to let go of her hair.

"I will go check on her. She did not sleep well last night. She tossed and turned all night. She may just be tired." Vayne sat the fish on the porch and went inside. He climbed the stairs and went into the bedroom to find Faith lying on the bed. He reached over, touched her back. She rolled over and smiled.

"I am so tired. I just need to take a nap." She yawned.

"I noticed you did not sleep well last night. You moved all night long. Were you having bad dreams?"

"No, just could not get comfortable. Not sure why," she said.

"You rest and I will fry up the fish I caught today. When you wake up, you might feel better, and you can eat."

Faith went to sleep, when she woke hours later, she felt a little better. She got up and headed downstairs. Vayne had sent everyone away, and he got up and brought her a plate of fish. When she looked at it, she ran from the plate, out the door and wretched. She came back in and sat down on the sofa. He put the cloth on her head. He leaned down and smiled.

"Why are you smiling, when I am sick?" She asked.

"Faith, when was the last time you had your cycle?" Vayne asked.

Faith sat up and looked at him. She could not remember. "I honestly do not know. I know I have not had it since father left. How long has he been gone?"

"He has been gone three months."

"Three months? You mean he has been gone that long. I have trouble keeping up with time here."

Vayne started laughing. He had suspected the last month that she might be expecting. After Maw Sally asked him had he noticed a glow, it hit him that was she was insinuating. *That old woman! You cannot get anything passed her!*

"Faith, I suspect you are with child." Vayne said calmly.

"Really? You really think that could be it. It would make sense because I have been tired, dizzy and when I saw that fish, it just made me ill. You don't think anything is wrong do you?"

Vayne smiled, "Oh everything is just right. Everything is perfect! We are going to have us a baby! We are going to have a baby!" Vayne picked her up and swung her around the room.

"Oh, my sweet Faith. Do not worry. Everything is perfect!"

Faith could hardly contain herself. *I am pregnant. I have wanted this and now it is happening. How could I have not thought of this? The dizziness, not sleeping well, tired. It was right in front me the entire time. I cannot believe I am finally with child. Ebony was right.*

It was now October; she would be due around April, if her calculations were correct. A spring baby would be perfect timing.

"We have so much to get ready. We need a crib, clothes, and blankets." Faith said.

"I have something to show you." Vayne got her hand and lead her to the stairs, and they went upstairs to the room that they always said would be a nursery. "I have been working on something for a couple of months. I will be honest with you, I suspected you were with child, but did not want to say anything." He opened the door and to her amazement, there was a crib in the room with a rocking chair. Vayne had been working on these and made them by hand.

'Trent helped me build these when he could. He knew what I suspected, as he had suspected you were with child also. I did not want to get your hopes up or mine either."

Faith walked over to the crib and ran her fingers over the wood. It was smooth to the touch and felt soft. "Vayne it is beautiful. How did you find the time to do this?"

"Some of those days I was fishing, I was working on this down by the beach." He smiled.

"This is the most beautiful thing I have ever seen, besides you." Faith wiped tears from her eyes.

Vayne wrapped his arms around her from behind, "I would do anything for you. When you are happy, I am happy."

"All this feels like a dream. I have never been so happy. Since the first day I met you, my life has only gotten better." Faith said as she turned toward him.

"Mine has to sweetheart. I never thought I was the settling down type. Once I met you, I did not want to anything, but settle down and just be with you." Vayne reached down and kissed her.

"Now, I do believe we have an announcement to make Mrs. Lafitte."

They walked downstairs so that they could share the good news.

Everyone was so excited about the coming of a new bundle of joy. The winter on the island was a mild one. Vayne had everything ready for winter, before it arrived. Everyone had what he or she needed for the winter months. Firewood, water, good and winter clothes and blankets. They all made a point to get together on Sundays so that they everyone could visit. Vayne and Faith kept little Rosie and Jean, until Faith got too far along with the baby, and it was too hard for her. They stayed in the cabin mostly in the winter. Vayne found that he desired Faith as much when she was pregnant, if not more, as when she was not with child. He loved to rub every inch of her, especially her round belly.

"When you talk, the baby moves more." Faith said to Vayne.

Vayne smiled, "She is going to be a daddy's little princess."

Faith leaned up on her elbow and looked at Vayne, "You never know. It might be a mommy's boy."

Vayne laughed, "You could be right. If it's healthy, I don't care if it's a girl or a boy."

"Me to." Faith said. She did not mind her big belly; it reminded her of the miracle growing inside of her. Vayne made her feel beautiful every day. He still wanted her physically exactly like has already had. She felt as if she wanted him more now, but she would never tell him that. Christmas came and went, and spring was fast approaching.

Everyone was glad that the winter months were over and done. Everyone enjoyed being out and enjoying the nicer weather. It was still cool at night, but Faith welcomed the cool. She did not mind the winter. She liked being in the cabin with Vayne and them enjoying their time together. She treasured all this time they had alone. She knew once the baby came, it would be three of them then. She looked forward to it, but also wanted to enjoy what time they had together without the baby as much as she could.

As Faith got bigger in the pregnancy, she was more uncomfortable and her huge belly made it hard for her to get around. They had moved downstairs, so that she would not have to climb the stairs. Vayne knew that the time was approaching for the baby. It could be any day, just a matter of time. So he would not leave her side. He remembered that Trent wasn't there at the births of his children due to illness and so Vayne helped Daisy. He was determined to be there for his child's arrival.

It was in the wee hours of the morning when Faith felt the first pang of tightening. She woke up and knew the pain she felt was different. She decided not to awaken Vayne quite yet. She wanted to see what happened. She didn't want to wake him for a false alarm. A few minutes later, she felt her stomach tighten again. She got up for some water and as she was walking back to bed, another pain started. She made it to the bed and sat down.

"Vayne?"

"Hhmmmmmmmm," Vayne rolled over to wrap his arms around her.

"Vayne," She said a little louder.

He sat up, "Everything okay?"

"I don't know. I am having some pain. My stomach is tightening and cramping." She said, as another one started.

"Let's get you back into bed. I will go and get Daisy. She can help you and she will be able to help me."

"Help you?" Faith looked at him.

"Yes ma'am. You did not think that I was going to let you deliver these babies without my help did you?" Vayne said as he got up out of bed.

Faith smiled.

"I will be back, do not do anything until I get back." Vayne smirked.

"Well, I am not sure I can help it if it happens, Mr. Lafitte."

"I will make it quick!" At that, he ran out of the cabin. He ran toward Trent and Daisy's Cabin, jump the fence and pounded on the door.

Daisy opened the door, "I need you to come quick. I believe that Faith is in labor and we are going to need your help" Vayne said out of breath.

"Oh my! I will be right behind you!" Daisy said.

Vayne made it back to the cabin and then Daisy was not far behind him. By the time they got back, Faith was sweating and breathing hard.

"I do believe this is it!" She said.

Daisy took her hand, "Vayne, you go heat up some water."

Vayne set about getting the water heated and got blankets and clothes. He could hear Faith's breathing getting faster. *Lord, please let her be okay. Please let her be okay. Please.*

"Just breathe Faith," Daisy said.

Vayne held her hand and sat in the bed with her. He rubbed her forehead with a wet cloth.

"I need to push! I need to push! I need to push!" Faith screamed.

Daisy got at the end of the bed, pulled back her gown, and could see the baby crowning.

"Yes you do need to push Faith. Go ahead and push." Daisy and looked up at Vayne. "You want to be the one to bring the baby into this world?"

Vayne got up and knelt at the end of the cot, "Push Faith, I see our baby right now! You have to push! "

Faith pushed, then pushed again and the third push, the baby was out.

Vayne, caught his daughter. "Faith, we have a beautiful daughter. Oh, she is beautiful. She is perfect."

Vayne cleared the baby's mouth, rubbed her belly and the first scream echoed through the cabin. He laid the baby on Faith's chest the mother daughter bond was immediate. Faith's heart melted, the baby nestled into her neck and stopped crying immediately. Vayne felt as if his heart would explode from the love he felt. His beautiful wife had given him a beautiful daughter. He had all he needed, right here in this little cabin.

Chapter 28
Three Years Later

Faith called. "Ebony! It is time for lunch."

"I'm coming mama. I was helping daddy with the fish." Ebony said.

"Ebony, when you were born you was a little princess. The most beautiful little baby your daddy and I had ever seen. Now all you want to do is fish and catch toads!" Faith said shaking her head.

Faith was round with child. She was due any day now. She looked at her daughter. She had dark hair like her daddy and green eyes like Faith. She was a perfect mixture of both of her parents and was as stubborn as her daddy was if you asked Faith. If you asked Vayne, she was stubborn like her mama.

Vayne entered the cabin, wrapped his arms around Faith, and gave her a kiss,

"Gross." Ebony curled her nose.

"Little girl, you are too smart for your own good. That will come in handy when you mama has the baby. She will need your help. Are you up for that?" Vayne asked as he sat down at the table.

"I am a big girl. I will be a big sister and a big helper," Ebony said.

"I never had a doubt you would be. Do you want to go help me at the light house when we finish lunch?" Vayne asked.

"Yes sir. I am almost done." Ebony popped the last piece of her biscuit into her mouth.

"Well, let's go. We will give mama some alone time so that she can rest," Vayne picked Ebony up and put her on his shoulders. They walked to the lighthouse. Ebony liked to go to the lighthouse and watch the birds at sea. The glass mesmerized her. She did not understand how it all worked.

As they got to the lighthouse, Vayne got her down off his shoulders and sat on the ground looking out at the ocean. Ebony crawled into his lap.

"Daddy please tell me the story about grandmother again. It is my favorite."

Vayne adjusted little Ebony on his legs, wrapped his arms around her, leaned his head next to hers and started his story, "Once upon a time, there was a Native American Warrior Princess named Ebony."

About the Author

A. D. Whittington grew up in a small, rural town in Alabama. She graduated in 1995 and moved to Mobile, AL in 1996. She has five children. Three boys and two adopted daughters. She resides in a small town in Mississippi with her husband, her youngest three children, and their two dogs. She started her first novel in high school, but out of fear of failure, she set it to the side and did not work on it again until 2018.

She did not stop writing entirely, she has had various poems published throughout the years, but her passion is writing stories. She likes to make her books her own and go outside of the box in her writing style. She decided in her forties that fear was no longer an option and decided to show her children that anything is possible. She wanted to leave a tangible legacy for her children and grandchildren.

A. D. wants everyone to know that if a country girl from Southern Alabama can make her dreams come true, so can you. You can keep up with A. D. Whittington on Facebook at:

https://www.facebook.com/AuthorDawnCarr/

Dear Readers:

I hope you have enjoyed this two-part novel as much as I did writing it. As authors, we strive to keep you entertained and we value your feedback. If you would do me a huge favor and go to Amazon and leave me an honest review, I really would appreciate it.

Best regards,
Dawn Carr

www.ingramcontent.com/pod-product-compliance
Lightning Source LLC
Chambersburg PA
CBHW031639040426
42453CB00006B/152